'There is a dignity inherent i~ ⌐   ng
that both challenges and   is
book addresses the core q   t
do Jesus' death and resurre   ..eristic
hope and a sense of advent   williams urges us
to take seriously the interpretations of the past while
remaining resolutely rooted in our own present, orien-
tated towards the future. We are asked to consider in this
book nothing less than the fundamental meaning of life
itself. And it is thanks to the genius of his scholarship that
the question brings joy in the answering.'

Lucy Winkett, Rector of St James's Church, Piccadilly

'Theology at its very best, and easily accessible too! Reading the book, I found myself drawn afresh to the vision of
"perfect humanity" made manifest in Jesus Christ.'

Miroslav Volf, Professor of Systematic Theology
Yale Divinity School

'This is a wonderful book: it is life-changing. No one can
read it without coming closer to the crucified and risen
Jesus . . . Rowan Williams is a very great teacher. With sim-
plicity, subtlety, profound seriousness and humour too,
he opens up to us the infinite depth of our Christian faith.'

Sister Wendy Beckett

'Rowan Williams is one of the great theologians of our
time. He is also an inspiring teacher whose godly wisdom
helps us to understand profound truths.'

Nicky Gumbel, Vicar of Holy Trinity Brompton
and pioneer of the Alpha Course

Born in 1950, Rowan Williams was educated in Swansea (Wales) and Cambridge. He studied for his theology doctorate in Oxford, after which he taught theology in a seminary near Leeds. From 1977 until 1986, he was engaged in academic and parish work in Cambridge, before returning to Oxford as Lady Margaret Professor of Divinity. In 1990 he became a fellow of the British Academy.

In 1992 Professor Williams became Bishop of Monmouth, and in 1999 he was elected as Archbishop of Wales. He became Archbishop of Canterbury in late 2002 with ten years' experience as a diocesan bishop and three as a primate in the Anglican Communion. As archbishop, his main responsibilities were pastoral – whether leading his own diocese of Canterbury and the Church of England, or guiding the Anglican Communion worldwide. At the end of 2012, after ten years as archbishop, he stepped down and moved to a new role as Master of Magdalene College, Cambridge.

Professor Williams is acknowledged internationally as an outstanding theological writer and teacher as well as an accomplished poet and translator. His interests include music, fiction and languages.

GOD WITH US

The meaning of the cross and resurrection – then and now

Rowan Williams

First published in Great Britain in 2017

Society for Promoting Christian Knowledge
36 Causton Street
London SW1P 4ST
www.spck.org.uk

British Library Cataloguing-in-Publication Data
A catalogue record for this book is available from the British Library

ISBN 978–0–281–07664–2
eBook ISBN 978–0–281–07665–9

1 3 5 7 9 10 8 6 4 2

Typeset by Graphicraft Limited, Hong Kong
First printed in Great Britain by Ashford Colour Press

eBook by Graphicraft Limited, Hong Kong

Produced on paper from sustainable forests

Contents

Part 1
THE MEANING OF THE CROSS

Part 2
THE MEANING OF THE RESURRECTION

Part 1

THE MEANING OF
THE CROSS

1

The sign

For to this you have been called, because Christ also suffered for you, leaving you an example, so that you should
follow in his steps. 'He committed no sin, and no deceit
was found in his mouth.' When he was abused, he did not
return abuse; when he suffered, he did not threaten; but
he entrusted himself to the one who judges justly. He
himself bore our sins in his body on the cross, so that,
free from sins, we might live for righteousness; by his
wounds you have been healed.   (Peter 2.21–24, NRSV)

When we go into a Christian place of worship, we expect
to see a cross. And when crosses are removed from public
places, such as crematoria or hospital chapels, we quite
reasonably get rather indignant about it. But in the world
in which Christianity began, a place of worship was the
last place you would expect to see a cross. We can only
begin to get some sense of what it might have felt like
to encounter the symbol of a cross in the first couple of
Christian centuries if we imagine coming into a church
and being faced with a large picture of an electric chair,
or perhaps a guillotine. The cross was a sign of suffering,
humiliation, disgrace. It was a sign of an all-powerful

3

empire that held life very cheap indeed: a forceful and immediate reminder to everybody that their lives were in the hands of the state. You might well be used to seeing crosses on the outskirts of towns or by the side of the road, but most definitely not in any place of worship.

When Jesus was a small boy there was a revolt in Galilee that was brutally suppressed by the Romans. We're told that there were thousands of crosses by the roads of Galilee. When in the Gospels Jesus speaks of picking up your cross and following him, he is not using a religious metaphor for things becoming a bit difficult.

So a group of people who proclaimed that the sign of their allegiance was a cross had a lot of explaining to do; and so we will be looking at some of the ways in which the first Christians tried to explain themselves. Because once we get past the surface level of being used today to seeing crosses around as a religious symbol, once we let ourselves recognize what it is that we are looking at, we are bound to be faced with some of the same questions. What is this about? How does it work? Why do we have an instrument of torture at the centre of our imagination?

The early Christians must have felt that they had no option but to talk about the cross. They knew that because of the death of Jesus on the cross their universe had changed. They no longer lived in the same world. They expressed this with enormous force, talking about a new creation, about liberation from slavery. They talked about the transformation of their whole lives and they pinned it down to the events that we remember each Good Friday. They couldn't get away from the cross – or so at least the New Testament seems to imply. There are in fact some New Testament scholars who try to argue that reflection on the cross of Jesus came in a little bit later. First came Jesus the charismatic teacher, the wandering prophet; first came an interest in his words rather than his deeds or his sufferings. And yet, when you read the earliest texts of Christian Scripture, not only the Gospels, it's difficult to excavate any stratum of thinking that is, as you might say, 'pre-cross'. Pretty well everything we read in the New Testament is shadowed by the cross. It is, first and foremost, the *sign* of how much has changed and how it has changed.

Even non-Christians in the world around recognized the central importance of the cross to Jesus' early followers. The earliest picture we have of the crucifixion is scratched on a wall in Rome; it may be as old as the second century. It is a rather shocking image: a man with a donkey's head strapped and nailed to a cross, and next to the cross a very badly drawn little figure wearing the short tunic of a slave, and scribbled above it, 'Alexamenos worshipping his god'. Presumably one of Alexamenos's fellow slaves had scrawled this little cartoon on the wall to make fun of him. But he knew, as Alexamenos knew, that Alexamenos' god was a crucified God.

The first Christians had some explaining to do; and so do we. In one of the great Christian poems of the twentieth century (the second of the *Four Quartets*), T. S. Eliot writes, 'Again, in spite of that, we call this Friday good.' That's the agenda for our reflections in this chapter: why is this instrument of suffering and death a sign of what is good?

The early Christians were at a huge disadvantage. They claimed that the world had changed because somebody had been executed by a death normally reserved for slaves and rebels. They were saying that their new life depended on somebody who had been so much at odds with the Roman world that the full force of the empire had crushed him. That might not in itself have been fatal if it had been possible to say that he died because he was defending his nation and his faith. In the couple of centuries just before the birth of Jesus, the Jewish people had begun to develop theories about martyrdom. They had come to believe that when somebody died for the law and for the nation, that person's death was pleasing to God: there's a phrase from a text of that time, affirming that 'God considers the soul of a man to be a worthy sacrifice.' But Jesus did not die defending the nation or the law against foreign oppression. He died because those who ruled his nation had collaborated with the oppressor. The early

Christians were thus caught in a sort of pincer movement: here was somebody condemned by the state and rejected by the religious authorities of his own people. So, imagine you're an early Christian and this is your sign. What is it a sign of?

Sign of God's love and freedom

Several times in the New Testament we encounter a phrase like 'God demonstrates' or 'proves' his love for the world by or through the cross. It's there, for example, in Romans 5.8: 'Christ died for us . . . and that is God's own proof of his love towards us.' We find similar language in 1 Timothy 2 and several times in the first letter of John. God has 'proved' his love for us through Jesus, and particularly through the death of Jesus. The Gospel of John goes even further, speaking of the death of Jesus as his 'glorification': when Jesus dies God's glory becomes fully manifest. So the execution of Jesus is a proof that God loves us, and so is also a demonstration of the *kind* of God that we are talking about. In John 12 Jesus says: 'When I am lifted up, I will draw everyone to me' – and the context makes it clear that his hearers are puzzled and shocked by the allusion to crucifixion. This is how the early Christians begin to push back at the expectations, you might almost say the clichés, of the world around. Yes, the cross is our sign and it is a sign of the kind of God we believe in.

How then does the execution of Jesus show the love of God? How does it become that sort of sign? We have a hint in Luke 23.34 and in the first letter of Peter 2.23. In Luke, as Jesus is crucified he says, 'Father, forgive.' And in Peter's letter we are reminded that when Jesus is abused he doesn't retaliate: 'When they hurled their insults at him, he did not retaliate.' Here is a divine love that cannot be defeated by violence: we do our worst, and we still fail to put God off. We reject, exclude and murder the one who bears the love of God in his words and work, and that love continues to do exactly what it always did. The Jesus who is dying on the cross is completely consistent with the Jesus we have followed through his ministry, and this consistency shows that we can't deflect the love that comes through in life and death. So when Pilate and the High Priest – acting on behalf of all of us, it seems – push God in Jesus to the edge, God in Jesus gently but firmly pushes back, doing exactly what he always did: loving, forgiving, healing.

So the cross is a sign of the transcendent freedom of the love of God. This is a God whose actions, and whose

The cross is a sign of the transcendent freedom of the love of God

reactions to us, cannot be dictated by what we do. You can't trap, trick or force God into behaving against his character. You can do what you like: but God is God. And if he wants to love and forgive then he's going to love and forgive whether you like it or not, because he is free. Our lives, in contrast, are regularly dominated by a kind of emotional economics: 'I give you that; you give me this.' 'I give you friendship; you give me friendship.' 'You treat me badly, and I'll treat you badly.' We're caught up in cycles of tit-for-tat behaviour. But God is not caught up in any cycle: God is free to be who he decides to be, and we can't do anything about it.

And that's the good news: the good news of our powerlessness to change God's mind. Which is just as well, because God's mind is focused upon us for mercy and for life. God will always survive our sin, our failure. God is never exhausted by what we do. God is always there, capable of remaking the relationships we break again and again. That's the sign of the cross, the sign of freedom.

It's out of that aspect of the New Testament – one strand among several – that the tradition arises in Christian history that has sometimes been called 'exemplarism': the cross of Christ is an example. 'Christ . . . suffered for you, leaving you an example,' says 1 Peter 2.21. Jesus was free from the vicious circle of retaliation, and so can we be and so should we be. Christ did not retaliate, return abuse for abuse; so neither should we. In the Acts of the Apostles we see that the free forgiveness of Jesus on the cross is already shaping the response of the disciples, because when

Stephen – the first martyr – faces his execution, he says something very similar to what Jesus says. What Jesus said to the Father, Stephen says to Jesus: 'Do not hold this sin against them' (Acts 7.60). Already, it seems, the way in which Jesus died on the cross has become a model that Christian believers must follow. And so, if we imitate the non-violent, non-retaliatory response of Jesus, we ourselves become a sign of the same divine love. We in our lives, in our willingness to be reconciled, show the world what kind of God we believe in: a God who is free from the vicious circle of violence and retaliation.

But it's not only that. The cross is an example *to* us but also an example *for* us. It is, in the old sense of example, a 'sample' of the love of God. This is what the love of God is like: it is free and therefore it is both all-powerful and completely vulnerable. All-powerful because it is always free to overcome, but vulnerable because it has no way of guaranteeing worldly success. The love of God belongs to a different order, not the order of power, manipulation and getting on top, which is the kind of power that pre-occupies us. This takes us a bit

This is what the love of God is like: it is free and therefore it is both all-powerful and completely vulnerable

beyond what the New Testament says in so many words, but only a bit. It's a very natural way for the idea to develop, and it's been very powerful in much Christian thinking. It allows us to say that the love of God is the kind of love that identifies with the powerless; the kind of love that appeals to nothing but its own integrity, that doesn't seek to force or batter its way through. It lives, it survives, it 'wins' simply by being itself. On the cross, God's love just is what it is and it's valid and world-changing and earth-shattering, even though at that moment what it means in the world's terms is failure, terror and death.

This has always been for Christians a hugely powerful idea: the defencelessness of the love of God, a love which has nothing but itself to rely on and yet somehow is all powerful. The weakness of God, said Paul, is stronger than human strength (1 Corinthians 1.25). And such a love – so many Christians have said – draws us towards Jesus. It has a magnetic force because it is a love that can't threaten us. How could we say no?

One of the people who most fully developed and reflected on this aspect of the cross was the twelfth-century philosopher and theologian Peter Abelard. He taught for many years in the schools of Paris, met with terrible personal tragedy and disaster, and ended his life as a monk. And it was he who first dwelt at length on the idea that the death of Jesus on the cross exemplifies a love that, when we have seen how it works, we simply can't refuse. One of the great novels of the twentieth century dealing with the Christian faith is Helen Waddell's *Peter Abelard*, a book in which Helen Waddell, a formidable scholar of the Middle Ages, seems to get right into the mind and the heart of Peter Abelard and of his lover and wife Eloise, and of the people around them – so much so that you really feel you are in Paris in the twelfth century and, yes, this must have been what they said to each other.

I'd like to dwell on two moments from that book. One is when Peter, in disgrace and deep despair, is trying to rebuild his life out in the country, having built a little hermitage. One of his former students is living alongside him, helping him with practical work and joining him at the altar. One day they're coming back from fishing and they hear a terrible cry, like a child's cry, coming from the woods behind them. They rush in the direction of the cry and find that it's not a child, it's a rabbit caught in a trap, squealing its life away in terrible anguish. They prise open the trap, the rabbit nestles its head for a moment in the crook of Peter's arm, and dies. And Peter feels for that moment overwhelmed by the sheer horror of the suffering that runs right through the world: his own suffering, the suffering he's inflicted on his wife, the suffering of this innocent animal. And to his amazement it's the student, Thibault, who has something to say to him.

'I think,' says Thibault nervously, 'God is in it too.'

Abelard looked up sharply.

'In it? Do you mean that it makes Him suffer, the way it does us?'

Again Thibault nodded.

'Then why doesn't He stop it?'

Thibault points to a tree near them:

That dark ring there, it goes up and down the whole length of the tree. But you only see it where it is cut across. That is what Christ's life was; the bit of God that we saw . . . We think God is like that for ever, because it happened once, with Christ. But not the pain. Not the agony at the last. We think that stopped.

> (Helen Waddell, *Peter Abelard*,
> London, Constable 1933, p. 270)

Abelard asks whether he means that 'all the pain of the world was Christ's cross' and Thibault says yes. The cross is the one moment when we see God and suffering brought together: but in fact it goes all the way through. Abelard is for a moment baffled and then intensely excited: 'O God, if it were true . . . it would bring back the whole world.'

Like a good academic he goes off to write a book about it, and unsurprisingly the book gets him into trouble. At the very end of the novel, we catch a glimpse of his continuing struggles with ideas, with prayer and with God. But this time we see him from a distance. We're back in

Paris in the room of the old Canon of Notre Dame, Gilles, who has been a great friend to him in the past: an old and cynical and pleasure-loving man who still has a deeply kind heart. And with him is Eloise, mistress and then wife of Peter, and now the deeply respected and beloved abbess of her own monastery. She and Peter have exchanged some correspondence but it hasn't really got anywhere. She still cannot quite see why he has gone the way he has and why they had to part, why all the pain. And Gilles tells her that he's had a letter from Peter.

'Does he speak of me?' asks Eloise. 'Not yet', Gilles replies. Eloise turns away to the window and when she turns round she sees a sight she had never expected to see, the old canon in tears. She goes to Gilles: 'Don't, Gilles. Beloved, you must not . . . It is over now. It doesn't hurt now.' She catches herself and says, 'Did you hear what I just said? . . . I can bear it now, because – because of you . . . Though why it should be – why you must break your heart to comfort mine . . .' Gilles looks at her, 'the old speculative gleam kindling in his eyes', and says, 'I wonder. Is that what men have asked of God?' (p. 282)

This takes us, I think, very close to the heart of why for many Christians the cross is a compelling sign not only of an inexhaustible love but of a *vulnerable* love. 'If it were true . . . it would bring back the whole world.' And it's strange and rather surprising to find the most orthodox and conventional thinker of the Middle Ages, the great St Thomas Aquinas, over a hundred years after Abelard, saying something very similar at one point. 'The cross,' says Aquinas, 'prompts us to love, and it is by this that we are forgiven.' The cross is what creates in us friendship with God. Here then is a very powerful and moving and resourceful tool for thinking about the cross. The sign of disgrace and exclusion, the sign of failure, is turned inside out to be a sign of that unique freedom which is God's freedom to be God whatever we do. But it is also a sign of the riskiness, the vulnerability, which such freedom must mean.

Sign of God's forgiveness

And yet, it has never been the whole of Christian thinking about the cross. Why not? If the cross were only an example of wonderful human behaviour, if the cross only said to us we should be ready to suffer nobly for our convictions or we should be non-violent and non-retaliatory, that would be and is inspiring, challenging (and alarming). But it doesn't yet tell us quite why the cross has anything to do with the forgiveness of sins. So that alone can't quite be all there is to it, in terms of the New Testament's assumptions. Even with the cross as an example or 'sample' of God's love drawing humankind towards Jesus, if this is just saying that the cross makes or might make us change our minds – does this quite do justice to the idea of a new creation, a new horizon for all our lives, new possibilities created within us, without our knowing or thinking about it?

The New Testament seems to want to say more. Perhaps more to the point, Jesus himself seems to want to say more. 'The Son of Man did not come to be served but to serve,' says Jesus in Mark 10.45, 'and to give his life as a ransom,' a payment, something that releases prisoners and hostages from their bonds. He came to give his life as a transaction, not just as an example but an act that some-

The cross effects a change that happens independently of our efforts or ideas

how springs the trap prior to any action or recognition of ours. The cross effects a change that happens independently of our efforts or ideas: the possibility of a deeply radically altered relationship with God, that doesn't depend on us.

So to speak of the cross as 'sign' is one of the most immediately and emotionally powerful ways in. Yet it isn't the only or the most comprehensive way of speaking. Every time we try to speak about how the cross works, we're saying something lying on a spectrum between two extremes. At one extreme is a very stark, objective idea: God does something and that's it. At the other extreme is subjectivity: we feel differently because of this event. In the Bible and in all Christian language and practice, these belong together. But the way in which people reflect on it all swings towards one end or the other of the spectrum. And what I've been speaking about in this chapter belongs at the more subjective end: what the cross causes us to feel, the difference made to how we think about God and ourselves and our world.

> When I survey the wondrous cross
> On which the Prince of glory died,
> My richest gain I count but loss
> And pour contempt on all my pride.

The writer of that hymn is looking at the cross, the sign of a 'love so amazing, so divine [that it] demands my soul, my life, my all'. But does everything depend on my ability to give 'my life, my soul, my all'? And is it really true that what the cross signifies is irresistible to human beings, automatically bringing back the whole world? It doesn't look like it, given the history of the world. Not so simple, surely. Yet so often it is this 'sign' element that most speaks to people, that addresses our fears and breaks down our defences, that *proves* to us (to go back to that aspect of New Testament language) that we needn't be afraid of God and that we needn't suffer alone in despair. A sign is something that communicates, that changes the world of meaning that we live in. It's a tangible word, a word that is expressed in an event, a symbol, a picture. And like other symbols and pictures it very often speaks to us at a level we can't fully make sense of. There have been many cases of people who, faced with the crucifix, can't ignore it or pass by.

There's a famous story from nineteenth-century France of a young military officer who made a bet with some of his colleagues. He was to go to confession in one of the big Paris churches and just pour out all the sins he could possibly think of to the priest in the most vivid and detailed terms. He did just that, thinking he'd been very clever. And on the other side of the grille there was a long silence and eventually the priest said, 'Now, my son, I want you to go back into the middle of the church in front of the big crucifix over the screen. I want you to look up at the crucifix and say, "You did that for me and I don't give a damn." And I want you to go on saying it as long as you can.' The young man went back and tried to do what he'd been instructed. He couldn't. He went off and joined a monastery. These are the levels at which the sign can work. So we mustn't imagine that because of the intellectual reservations there may be around this and the problems that they raise, we can easily let go of it.

A great twentieth-century French theologian said that in Holy Week, Jesus 'placed himself in the order of signs'. He made himself a symbol, a communication of God's love. And that's what we've been reflecting on in this chapter. Behind it and beyond it remains a mystery, a mystery that is in fact deeply connected with some of the themes we've already touched upon. If we're looking towards the freedom of the all-powerful God expressed in this failure and desolation, all kinds of images and ideas begin to unfold. And yet to think of the cross as the sign of freedom – God's freedom and therefore our freedom also – at least begins to clear the ground for thinking about some of the other images, the wealth of metaphor, that the rest of the New Testament brings to bear on the mystery.

For reflection or discussion

1 Try to imagine yourself as an early Christian believer. What might come into your mind when you think of the cross?
2 Do you find the idea that the cross is a sign of God's freedom helpful for your own life?
3 Have there been moments in your life when the cross has broken down your defences?

2

The sacrifice

Since the law has only a shadow of the good things to come and not the true form of these realities, it can never, by the same sacrifices that are continually offered year after year, make perfect those who approach. For it is impossible for the blood of bulls and goats to take away sins . . . Consequently, when Christ came into the world, he said,

'Sacrifices and offerings you have not desired,
but a body you have prepared for me;
in burnt-offerings and sin-offerings
you have taken no pleasure.
Then I said, "See, God, I have come to do your will, O God"
(in the scroll of the book it is written of me).'

When he said above, 'You have neither desired nor taken pleasure in sacrifices and offerings and burnt-offerings and sin-offerings' (these are offered according to the law), then he added, 'See, I have come to do your will.' He abolishes the first in order to establish the second. And it is by God's will that we have been sanctified through the offering of the body of Jesus Christ once for all.

(Hebrews 10.1, 4–10, NRSV)

We noted in the previous chapter that there doesn't seem to be any stage in the history of Christian thinking when the cross is not an issue. There is no pre-cross Christianity. This is shown by (among other things) certain turns of phrase that you find in various places in the New Testa-

There is no pre-cross Christianity

ment. One of those turns of phrase is that Jesus died 'for us' or 'for our sins' or 'for many' – for the multitude. You find phrases like that in the very earliest stratum of the New Testament – in the Gospel of Mark, where Jesus speaks of his life as a ransom for many (10.45), in the first letter of Peter, which talks of Jesus 'suffering once for sins, the righteous for the unrighteous' (3.18) and, in what's probably the oldest summary confession of faith in the New Testament, in 1 Corinthians 15.3–4: 'What I received I passed on to you as of first importance: that Christ died for our sins according to the scriptures, that he was buried, that he was raised on the third day according to the scriptures.'

Paul is saying unambiguously to his converts in Corinth, 'I'm telling you what they – the first generation of believers – told me, and they told me that Jesus died for our sins.' So not only is the first stratum, the base level, of Christianity preoccupied with the cross: it seems to take it for granted that the cross is *for* something, that it is an event whose effect is liberation given to us from beyond ourselves.

21

Quite a lot of Christian thought throughout the ages has veered towards talking about a kind of 'legal' element in the death of Christ. We deserve to be punished, Christ takes our punishment, and so we walk free out of the court. But while that language is there in some places in the New Testament, Paul's language and Peter's are probably not first and foremost about the law court, but about the Temple. If a first-century Jew had heard the statement that Jesus died 'for many', for the forgiveness of sins, his or her first thought would probably have been to connect it with the system of sacrifice: when blood is shed in God's presence, for the sake of God's people, for the avoiding of disaster, that is sacrifice. So the language of sacrifice is very deeply rooted in the New Testament and the rest of this chapter could easily be taken up going through the passages one by one to show the different ways in which this language is used. I'll try to condense it a little.

Sacrifice in the Old Testament

The problem is that already in the Old Testament there is a vast amount of material about sacrifice. It's not just one kind of thing. We may tend in our minds to have a rather simple idea of sacrifice in the ancient world: you kill an animal to get on the right side of a god. But in the Old Testament there's a great deal more than that going on. You might, for example, sacrifice in order – says Exodus 34 – to redeem or buy back your first-born son. Somehow the first arrival of a new generation is a life under threat, a life at risk; you need to 'buy back' that life into safety by offering a lamb in its place. Or then again you might turn to the book of Leviticus – a book full of immensely rich reflection on sacrifice. In chapter 3 we hear about the sacrifice that makes peace, in chapters 4–7 about the sacrifices that are to be offered to do away with guilt. And in chapter 16 we have the great dramatic ritual of the Day of Atonement explained to us, where the sins of the whole people are ceremonially laid on the head of a goat who is driven out into the wilderness – the scapegoat. In Leviticus 17.11 we read that the blood of a sacrificed animal 'covers over' sin or guilt, because 'the life of a creature is in the blood' and 'It is the blood that makes atonement for one's life'. In Numbers 15 we hear once more of sacrifices made for sin. And in Exodus 29 there is the commandment given to offer a lamb, morning and evening, day by day, in the Temple sanctuary. In the times between the end of the Old Testament and the beginning of the New Testament, Jewish thinkers seem to have begun to make the association of this daily offering of the lamb with the event that lay at the very beginning of Israel's history, when Abraham attempted to sacrifice Isaac on Mount Moriah and was prevented by God, who provided a ram (a male lamb, said the later scholars) for a sacrifice. It was believed that the

Temple in Jerusalem stood on the place where Abraham had tried to sacrifice Isaac, and so the morning and evening sacrifice of the lamb at the Temple in Jerusalem was a re-enactment of that first event when God had stepped in to provide a sacrificial victim in place of Isaac, the ancestor of the Jewish people.

We can begin to see just how much is going on in the language of sacrifice, and how very hard it is to push it all into a tidy system. If you look hard you'll find that Exodus, Leviticus and Numbers don't always give you the same commands for the same things, and that if you were trying to run a tightly organized sacrificial system on the basis of these texts alone, you'd have quite a lot of problems: though of course they operated such a system in the Temple in Jerusalem daily and, as far as we know, very successfully. But in the middle of it all is one great governing idea: a sacrifice is something given over into the hands of God, most dramatically when it is a life given over with the shedding of blood. That gift of life or blood somehow casts a veil over the sin or sickness or disorder of an individual or of a whole people. It removes the consequences of sin; it offers the possibility of a relationship unclouded by guilt with God; it is a gift that stands between God and the failures or disorders of the world. The gift is given – and it's a costly gift because it's about life and blood – so that peace and communication may be re-established between heaven and earth. And this was always symbolized by the fact that a sacrificed animal would be cooked and cut up and shared in the meal, which expressed not only fellowship with one another, but restored fellowship with God.

It's a gift that in the language of the Old Testament turns away the anger and displeasure of God. In the jargon of theology it 'propitiates' God, it makes things all right with him again, but also it brings him back into an active relationship with the world. At the highest point, sacrifice establishes – or re-establishes, confirms – the *covenant*, God's alliance with God's people. It's the sign of God's promise to be with the people. The gift is given, and in response God not only covers over sin but promises actively to be there for his people. The alliance, the treaty between God and God's people, is renewed. So again in Exodus (24.8) we read of 'the blood of the covenant' – the covenant between God and Israel, the covenant that Moses is establishing, is sealed with a sacrifice whose blood is sprinkled on the people.

Sacrifice in the New Testament

This is a world that we today don't find very easy or comfortable to inhabit. The idea of animal sacrifice is an oddity, perhaps an offensive one, and the idea that we give God gifts in order to calm him down doesn't sound quite like the God we know in the New Testament. And yet all the models that I've mentioned are at one point or another used by writers in the New Testament. Paul uses quite widely the language of propitiation, the gift that makes peace with God. He seems to refer to the Day of Atonement ritual, the scapegoat, and he certainly alludes in 1 Corinthians 11 to the 'blood of the covenant' because that's what he reports Jesus talking about at the Last Supper. The epistle to the Hebrews – which has a good claim to be the most complicated text in the New Testament – is an immensely sophisticated meditation on the Day of Atonement, and how Jesus has now performed a Day of Atonement ritual not just for one year but for ever.

Interestingly the first letter of Peter and the book of Revelation seem to be alluding to Abraham and Isaac and the ram, because of a turn of phrase that both use. Peter (1 Peter 1.19–20) speaks of the offering of a lamb which was foreseen before the world began. The book of Revelation (13.8) – on one reading of an admittedly ambiguous sentence – speaks of 'the Lamb who was slain from the creation of the world'. And this reflects another of those very rich Jewish interpretative traditions. Abraham prepares to sacrifice Isaac, but God is going to provide a lamb in Isaac's place. More to the point, God has *already* – from the creation of the world – made a lamb to be slaughtered on this occasion. On Mount Moriah, when Abraham tries to kill Isaac, God has already foreseen this action and has already created the lamb which is going to appear, mysteriously, on the mountain top. So when Peter and the author of Revelation speak of a lamb killed before the foundation of the world, they're almost certainly thinking of this reference back to Abraham and Isaac, what the Jewish sages call the Akedah, the mystery of the binding of Isaac.

Bearing all that in mind, we can see that it's not at all easy to get a precise theory of Christ's death as sacrifice out of the New Testament. However, that said, I believe it's possible to identify at least three clear ways in which the New Testament writers saw Christ's death in terms of sacrifice.

First, they speak of the death of Jesus as a sacrifice because it's a rescue operation. Its purpose is to turn aside terror and catastrophe, pain, suffering, punishment. It breaks the chain between evil actions and evil consequences.

> *The death of Jesus breaks the chain between evil actions and evil consequences*

Second, the New Testament, like the Old Testament, takes it for granted that this catastrophe and terror is something that doesn't just face individuals – it affects the life of the whole community. Which is why when Jesus himself speaks of his life being given up to rescue 'many', he's referring to that aspect of sacrifice which deals with the failure and disorder, the injustice, of an entire nation (and in the background there too, of course, we can hear the words of Caiaphas the High Priest in John 11.50, 'It is better for you that one man die for the people than that the whole nation perish.'

Third, because of all this, sacrifice is a means of establishing and reinforcing the covenant. It seals the alliance, the peace treaty, between God and humanity. It brings afresh into the world the reality of God's committed relationship to this community and becomes the foundational event for a new kind of human living together.

So the New Testament is telling us that the death of Jesus is a rescue operation that averts catastrophe, but one that works not just on behalf of individuals, but on behalf of the whole community that God wants to gather. It tells us that it has something to do with bringing into the world the concrete and powerful truth that God is committed to those he calls.

Sacrifice as obedience

We may still be feeling a bit uncomfortable about all this language of blood and propitiation and 'calming God down'. Not surprisingly; this is language that takes for granted a picture of God that doesn't at first sight sit very well with the God of Jesus. But we sometimes forget that our Jewish and early Christian ancestors were not nearly as stupid or morally obtuse as we are tempted to think. They had already spotted the problems. The ancient Jews had identified it even before the time of the New Testament. They had already concluded that we can't talk in this way about calming God down and pouring out blood to keep God happy. This must be a symbol, a metaphor.

But what's it a metaphor *for*? In that very creative period between the Old and New Testaments the Jews had already begun to think – and you find it in the Old Testament itself – that the real heart of sacrifice was *obedience*. 'What's the greatest gift we could give to God? Our hearts, our wills, our decisions' – in other words, our obedience. Already in the Old Testament we hear in 1 Samuel 15.22 that 'To obey is better than sacrifice.' And we hear in some of the prophets of God's impatience with a system of sacrifice that does nothing to change people's behaviour. Again and again the prophets say to the people, 'You are expert at sacrificing things; why is it so hard to sacrifice yourselves?' And (with a strongly satirical turn), in Psalm 50.13 God says, 'Do I eat the flesh of bulls or drink the blood of goats?' So the Jews have already moved away from the literalism that embarrasses us. And in the period between the Testaments, the assimilation of obedience and sacrifice is widely developed. For the sages of this period, to perform the law faithfully and fully is to make an acceptable sacrifice. To perform the law, to do God's will, is to give God the gift that pleases him most.

I quoted in the last chapter a statement from a Jewish writer of that period: 'God considers the soul of a man to be a worthy sacrifice.' And this ideal of obedience was what was in the mind of that writer: we give our souls in perfect obedience to the law. Sometimes, as in the persecutions of that period, obedience to the law could mean death at the hands of a ruthless occupying power. But the basic point is simply that giving your heart to God is a sacrifice, and it's a sacrifice that, like the sacrifices in Leviticus, can cover over the sins of others.

Interestingly it's a tradition that has survived in the Jewish world. Some of you may have come across the haunting image in certain traditions of Judaism of the 36 Righteous People – the 36 Zaddikim – who in Hasidic Judaism are the people who in every generation keep the world going. We don't know who they are, but somehow in every generation there's somebody around whose virtue and prayer upholds the world itself, somebody whose life is such a perfect example of obedience that God says, 'I won't give up on the world yet.' We are all indebted to these 36 mysterious people whom we never know about, who are keeping the wrath of God at arm's length.

You can see how, against that background, the life and the death of Jesus begin to make slightly better sense;

because of course Jesus' death is *not* a ritual sacrifice. It doesn't happen in a temple, it happens on a bleak hilltop on an execution ground. Jesus' sacrifice is the sacrifice of obedience. At every moment of his life he has given his heart to God in such a way that God is able to work through him with no interruption, with no diversion. At every moment Jesus has fulfilled the law; not by ticking off at the end of every day a series of acts performed; not by obeying God like a reluctant corporal with a sergeant major ordering him around; but at every moment Jesus has done what God wants. So even before his crucifixion we could say in Jewish terms that he was offering a sacrifice, giving his heart to God in such a way that God is pleased with the gift.

But as with those martyrs in the period between the Testaments, it was an obedience that led to death. Jesus' single-minded gift of his heart to the Father leads him to the shedding of his blood, because obedience to God in this world of sin, oppression and violence puts you lethally at risk. This is a world in which if you try to give your heart to God you may find your blood shed; it's that kind of world. That's why the New Testament speaks of the cost of Jesus' obedience, and of Jesus paying a price on our behalf; he buys us back. The language is there in 1 Peter and Paul's letter to the Galatians and elsewhere. This life is paid over on the cross. It is given to God so that sins may be covered over, so that peace may be restored, and that means the paying of a price, a life, the shedding of blood.

Sacrifice as gift

Let's step back for a moment from this concentration on the language of sacrifice as risk and death. So far, we've seen that sacrifice is the gift that makes peace. We've seen how in the New Testament it's a way of creating the new community and pushing away the threat of catastrophe. We've seen how Jesus' life, understood as a life of total obedience, can be seen as a sacrifice up to and including his death. But there is another dimension to it which later Christian theology was to pick up and run with. One of those who most effectively did so was the great Anselm of Canterbury, who lived in the later eleventh and early twelfth century. What is the gift that most pleases God? Well, said theologians at the time, obedience, certainly; but actually what's pleasing in obedience is that God looks into our world and sees a reflection of his own love, his glory and his beauty there. Obedience is not springing to attention and hastily doing what you're ordered. Obedience is a harmony of response to God so that God sees in the world a reflection

> Obedience is a harmony of response to God so that God sees in the world a reflection of his own life

of his own life. Our actions in obedience reflect his. So to put it simply, what most pleases God is God. God loves to see his selfless love reflected, to see his beauty mirrored back to him. Thus the perfect gift to God, the gift that God would really like, is *God*, the return to him of his own wholly generous love.

If we turn to some other passages in the New Testament – the Gospel of John, 1 Corinthians, Colossians, Hebrews – we can already see Christians beginning to feel their way here towards a deeper mystery. The obedience that Jesus offers to his Father is not just that of a very pious Jew: it goes deeper. It's a loving gift which directly and uninterruptedly and perfectly reflects God's own loving gift. It's the Son watching what the Father does and 'playing it back' to him. That's the language of the fourth Gospel (5.19) where Jesus says that he does what he sees his Father doing. So Jesus' obedience becomes the way in which the love of the eternal God shines in Jesus' life and death back to God the Father: perfect harmony but in the gift of God and the response from the earth.

In Jesus there is the divine action of love mirrored back to God through the medium of a human life. And suddenly our thinking about sacrifice has taken us right into the middle of the doctrine of the Trinity and the doctrine of the Incarnation. Our language about sacrifice has shown us a God who is giving and receiving and responding. This is a God who pours out love and draws it back: a God who is himself relationship, not a solitary tyrant waiting for us to get on the right side of him. And the effect of the death of Jesus is to bring us into that everlasting relation-ship: the Father pouring out his love, the Son watching what the Father is doing and playing it back to him, the Spirit enabling us to share that response to the Father, watching and loving.

In the life of Jesus we see all of that vast infinite eternal reality happening in a human life, happening in a weary, dusty-footed unkempt man completing a long journey, sitting down with his friends at the end of the day, break-ing bread and pouring wine. That prosaic, everyday picture of Middle Eastern peasant life is where God happens in the world, where the love of God becomes absolutely real and active. And when that dusty-footed Galilean peasant is nailed and strapped to the beams of the cross then we say, yes, what we see is no less than the Holy Trinity: the life of God poured out, the life of God reflected back in love from the earth and the breathing of that life freely to the ends of creation, the Spirit of Jesus.

I think it was partly this kind of understanding which lay behind St Anselm's way of talking about the death of Jesus – and it's sometimes misunderstood. At the heart of his argument is the idea of giving a gift to God that is worthy of God. What gift could be worthy of God except

God's own love? Jesus, perfectly human, perfectly divine, gives it to God as we cannot because of our ingrained sin. So the life and death of Jesus are the translation into human terms of the eternal truth of God the Father, the Son and the Spirit. And when that divine life becomes active and local and immediate in the world, it changes the definition of what human beings are. It interposes between God and human failure, a new face for humanity.

'Look Father, look on his anointed face, and only look on us as found in him,' says the great eucharistic hymn. We are able to say to God: 'Don't look at our failures. You know, Lord God, that humanity is more than this because you have *made* it more than this. You know that humanity is more than me and my miserable and wretched and incompetent struggles to be human, because you have given to the world perfect humanity: Jesus' humanity. And in association with that new human nature I can be at peace with you, my sins forgiven, my injuries healed, a new creation.'

The absolute creative love of God has done what only God can do, and given a completely new start to the world, to you and me. And that's a change in human nature that doesn't depend on my efforts, or on my acquiring a lot of bright new ideas. It's done, it's happened; God has lived this life that breaks through the envelope of humanity, remakes and remoulds what it is to be human, and it's done by living that life of total giving to God – including failure and death. Jesus has cleared the ground for a new human nature. Remember how in the last chapter we were thinking about the way the cross as a sign told us that we didn't have to be trapped in the vicious circle of retaliation: when we think of the cross as sacrifice, however complex the ideas around it, what the language is trying to get us to see is that this new possibility is something objectively done for us, done on our behalf for us, for many, for our sins; which is where we began.

This is a deeply mysterious area. As we watch and listen to the writers of the New Testament struggling with this immense metaphor of sacrifice in all sorts of different contexts, we are likely to feel frustrated at the thought that there's so much there and we can't quite get a grip on it all. But it is saying that what Jesus does, who Jesus is, is a gift offered to God, offered from the earth, from humanity, and yet offered with divine liberty and divine love. That gift – so costly, so painful in a world of injustice and violence – 'covers over' the world's failure, makes the face of the world new, makes peace.

This means the consequences of living in a world of injustice and terror are not simply cancelled, but put in a new context. The catastrophe, the self-destructive spiral downwards of human beings, is grabbed and halted by the hand of God. Now there is something else possible, the catastrophe is turned away, the punishment is lifted because the gift has been given and a way has been opened. The writer of the letter to the Hebrews (10.20) calls this 'a new and living way that he opened for us' from where we are – the thorns, thickets and clouds, the storms of angry power and tormented minds, are somehow cleared. It's possible for us to be human again, to grow as we move along that living pathway to reconciliation with God and each other.

It wasn't surprising that the first Christians turned to the language of sacrifice. They knew that it wasn't straightforward, they knew the problems that we feel and they were often a lot more nuanced and sophisticated than many modern Christians when they talked about the cross. They knew that sacrifice was a vast and rich metaphor, and they couldn't think of any better way of understanding the obedience of Jesus. They certainly believed that Jesus suffered for us, indeed suffered in our place, that he drew to himself the consequences of human evil and sin, that he accepted for himself the terrible destructiveness of the human world and absorbed it in himself.

So we do have to think about what some people call the language of 'substitution', Jesus suffering 'in our place'. But we ought not to suppose that the only sensible language for talking about the cross is that of Jesus bearing our punishment. This is part of it, but not the whole. The world of sacrifice in the fuller sense that I've been trying to set out is arguably closer to the heart of the New Testament writers.

So, after thinking in Chapter 1 about the cross of Jesus as a *sign*, a powerful communication of who God is, we have moved a little bit along the spectrum I described, from subjectively focused considerations to something more independent of our response and understanding. We're moving to the point where we have to say that it's not about what I'm doing here, but about what God is doing. And in this connection, it's worth noting that in the Old Testament when we read about atonement, the subject of the verb 'to atone' is always humanity. Priests make atonement by performing sacrifices. But in the New Testament the subject is God. God makes peace with us, working through us, acting for us. It is God's act, outside us, not up to us; something that God has accomplished. Which is why, as we shall see in the next chapter, the New Testament also speaks of the cross in the language of *victory*.

For reflection or discussion

1 1 In what way do the images or passages on sacrifice, either from the Old Testament or the New Testament, inspire you?

2 How does Jesus' giving his heart to God as a sacrifice of obedience speak to you?

3 How does the doctrine of the cross as a gift renew you in your Christian life?

3

The victory

'Now my soul is troubled. And what should I say – "Father, save me from this hour"? No, it is for this reason that I have come to this hour. Father, glorify your name.' Then a voice came from heaven, 'I have glorified it, and I will glorify it again.' The crowd standing there heard it and said that it was thunder. Others said, 'An angel has spoken to him.' Jesus answered, 'This voice has come for your sake, not for mine. Now is the judgement of this world; now the ruler of this world will be driven out. And I, when I am lifted up from the earth, will draw all people to myself.' He said this to indicate the kind of death he was to die.   (John 12.27–33, NRSV)

In the oldest of the Gospels, we're told (Mark 15.37) that Jesus died with 'a loud cry'. But it is the author of the fourth Gospel who dares to gives a word to that cry. In John's Gospel (19.30) Jesus dies crying *tetelestai*, 'It is finished'; the work is completed.

That single word, *tetelestai*, carries within it a deep sense of the cross as *victory*. There has been a mortal struggle and Jesus has emerged victorious. It is typical of the fourth Gospel, and John has laid a trail for us already. In the twelfth chapter we have the imagery of the prince of this world being cast out: 'Now is the time for judgment on this world; now the prince of this world will be driven out. And I, when I am lifted up from the earth, will draw all people to myself' (John 12.31–32).

There is a struggle, and the prince of this world, the evil power that dominates humanity, is cast out, cast down or driven out. This language is repeated in John 14.30–31 where, once again, the victory, the completion of the struggle on the cross, is foreshadowed. Jesus says at the Last Supper,

> I will not say much more to you, for the prince of this world is coming. He has no hold over me, but he comes so that the world may learn that I love the Father and do exactly what my Father has commanded me. Come now, let us leave.

Here the struggle is impending, but the prince of this world is already foredoomed to fail. And in that last phrase Jesus summons his followers to witness the last battle. Similarly in 16.33, again at the Last Supper, 'In this world,' says Jesus to his friends, 'you will have trouble. But take heart! I have overcome the world.'

What all these texts in John's Gospel tell us is that the *cross* is a victory, because in a sense the victory has already been won in the *life* of Jesus. He has conquered, because he has at each moment given himself in unreserved love, dedication and obedience to God and to the needs of the world. The victory has already been won. And the outcome of the last struggle on Good Friday is, you might say, a foregone conclusion. For all the horror, the pain and the violence that surround that last episode, something has already been established in the character of Jesus' life that tells us what the result will be. And Jesus' acceptance of the cross as part of his obedience is the way in which he makes his *Passion* into an *action*: that is, the way in which he turns an experience in which he is passive, at the mercy of others, into something that is active and that allows God's own action to flood through into the world.

The victim becomes the victor

Tetelestai: 'it is finished', 'it is done with'. The cross is the seal on a particular kind of life: a life which has turned away from violence, manipulation, domination; a life in which the Son of Man is there not to be served but to serve; a life in which the very act of God is made flesh and blood in a vulnerable human being. Already in the life of Jesus we see that the quality and character of this life and this love are such that death is too small for it. That is why, when we turn to the last book of the Bible, to the Revelation of John, we find there many songs of victory, which are addressed to or which name God and 'the Lamb' together. God and the sacrificial victim, they are the ones to whom praise and worship is due because they, together, have won the victory. The Lamb who was slaughtered is worthy to receive praise. The Lamb has conquered. And in a set of very paradoxical and challenging images, the writer of Revelation underlines the oddity of what he's talking about. The Lamb, the helpless, woolly creature trussed and slaughtered on the butcher's slab, the Lamb becomes the triumphant conqueror. It is the Lamb who releases the enemy's prisoners, the Lamb who has led the ultimate successful raid into enemy territory and brought back the prisoners of death and evil. In Revelation 5.9, for example, the Lamb has won, has earned a cosmic triumph. Again in 5.13, the Lamb has conquered and has set us free. The victim has become the victor.

Turning back a little bit in the New Testament to the second chapter of the letter to the Colossians, we find some of the same language. By the cross Jesus has released us and bound the enemy. It's worth reading the very dense little passage that starts at 2.13:

> When you were dead in your sins and in the uncircumcision of your flesh, God made you alive with Christ. He forgave us all our sins, having cancelled the charge of our legal indebtedness, which stood against us and condemned us; he has taken it away, nailing it to the cross. And having disarmed the powers and authorities, he made a public spectacle of them, triumphing over them by the cross.

So the enemies of human creation are bound and humiliated. Like the captives of war they are dragged at the chariot wheels of the victorious commander. The language is nakedly that of the imperial triumphs in Rome. But note also that the word translated 'disarmed' literally means that Christ on the cross discards, sheds, throws off the weight of the powers that enslave us. As if slipping off a garment, Christ shrugs off the leaden weight of those powers that keep us less than human. And on the cross, as the body of Jesus is nailed there, so too is nailed, metaphorically, the account that his death has cancelled. He has written off our debt and when we look at him nailed there, what we see is all that we owe in fear and guilt nailed up, with a red line through it.

So, although the language of victory is perhaps not as widespread in the New Testament as that of sacrifice, you can see that it's certainly there, that it's used very vividly, and that it's used with what almost seems to be a mischievous sense of paradox. We may be used to singing about the triumphs of the slaughtered Lamb, but there is something almost comic about a Lamb as superhero, and I suspect the writer of Revelation must have known that.

> *We may be used to singing about the triumphs of the slaughtered Lamb, but there is something almost comic about a Lamb as superhero*

However, the underlying point is what I've already stressed. In accepting the cross, turning passion into action, Jesus has accepted in advance the risk of total loss and so exposed the depth and the scope of divine freedom, as we saw in our first chapter. Because of who he is, what he does and what he suffers, there can now be no obstacle in the path between humanity and God, as we saw in the second chapter. All that pretends to intrude between us and God is abruptly swept away. So any power or influence, any cosmic trend, any pattern of life that tries, so to speak, to shoulder its way between us and God – 'you must do this because I tell you to and I know what God wants' – becomes very suspect. Instead of this we are swept into Jesus' way of life, Jesus' liberty – which is more than law, which is grace drawing us into the very heart of the Holy Trinity. And so the kingdoms of this world become the kingdom of our God and of his Anointed (Revelation 11.15).

Now this language is of course associated at various points in the New Testament with the victorious event of the resurrection, as you would expect it to be. But I wanted to begin this chapter by stressing that it is also language about the cross – not just about the resurrection as a triumphantly happy ending. You'll find in Ephesians 4.8ff, a model of ascent and descent. The Saviour comes right down to the depths of the forsaken world and draws the whole complex of reality back up, home to God – leading a train of captives, leading the enemies of humanity, the diabolical powers, in the conqueror's procession (as in Colossians). But, for the author of Revelation, as for Paul in Colossians, the victory is *already* in the cross, and indeed *already* in the life. Life, death and resurrection are of a piece.

This is essential in thinking about the cross. From time to time, people say, 'Isn't it odd that Christianity so often seemed in earlier centuries to pass over the ministry and teaching of Jesus as if it's in a hurry to get to the cross.' In the creed nothing apparently happens between 'born of the Virgin Mary' and 'suffered under Pontius Pilate', whereas the Gospels make it plain that actually quite a lot happened. But perhaps all of this helps us a little bit to see how the cross is *not* an episode at the end of the life of Jesus but the coming to fulfilment of what that life has been about. This life of utter givenness to God and the other, the neighbour, is already a life that death cannot contain. And so we cannot understand the cross fully without understanding the life.

The victory is already in the cross, the victory is already in the life, and that also enables us to say that the resurrection, instead of being any kind of afterthought, displays what has always been true. The resurrection displays the integrity, the indestructibility, of the love that has been at work all through. The resurrection is neither an optional extra nor a happy ending, it is the inescapable bursting through of the essential reality of who and what Jesus is. Once we grasp in the full light of the resurrection whom this story is all about, then we see exactly what those disciples on the road to Emmaus saw. It was necessary. It all hangs together. The life that began in the womb of the Virgin Mary, which is worked out in the ministry in Galilee, which is apparently ended on the cross, which is released once again in the resurrection – it's one thing, one story.

> *The resurrection is neither an optional extra nor a happy ending, it is the inescapable bursting through of the essential reality of who and what Jesus is*

The cross of Christ as victor

From the beginning, language of the cross as victory was deeply attractive and powerful to the first Christians. The earliest pictures of the crucifixion (apart from that odd little cartoon I mentioned in Chapter 1) are images that are clearly of a Christ triumphant. The earliest depictions lay very little stress on the sheer human suffering, because those pictures are created by people seeing from the vantage point of resurrection what had been going on in the life and the death of Jesus. Not until about the tenth Christian century do you have anything you might call a realistic representation of the crucifixion. I don't think this is some kind of evasion, some kind of unwillingness to face the painful or embarrassing facts of Jesus' suffering. Right at the beginning, of course, people knew exactly what a crucified person looked like. And to depict a crucified person triumphant and free was not a bit of pious metaphor, but something immensely powerful, breaking through a stereotype.

But it's not only in pictures and carving and painting that this language appears. Some of the oldest Christian hymns use it also. Two of the greatest and best-known hymns of Passiontide come out of this tradition. Both were written by a bishop in Roman Gaul just as Roman political power was receding across the Alps, Bishop Venantius Fortunatus. 'The royal banners forward go, the cross shines forth in mystic glow.' To sing that hymn for the first time each successive year is for many of us the real beginning of the Passion season. And then there is the great Good Friday hymn, 'Sing my tongue the glorious battle, sing the ending of the fray.' Venantius knew what a Roman legion looked like – and he knew what Roman legionaries' marching songs sounded like. He wrote these hymns in the dogged, plodding metre of soldiers' marching songs. Vex*illa re*gis *prod*e*unt,* ful*get* cruc*is* my*sterium.* Listen to them, the patter of anything but tiny feet, in standard issue legionary boots, along the roads of Gaul.

Pange lingua gloriosi, another determined, plodding metre that would greatly have upset any classical Latin writer: marching songs for the Christian army.

(As an aside, there's a very odd phrase in 'The royal banners' which some of you will have noticed. 'Fulfilled is all that David told/ in full prophetic song of old./ Among the nations, God, said he,/ hath reigned and triumphed from the tree.' Many people must have wondered where exactly David said that, in his true prophetic songs – i.e. the psalms. And the answer is, that in the Greek Old Testament somebody mistranslated the phrase 'The Lord is king' (straightforward enough) as 'The Lord has reigned' and for some reason the Greek translator added the words *apo xylo,* 'from the wood' or 'from the tree'. No one's absolutely sure what he thought he was doing. It may be that he picked up the Hebrew word *selah* in the psalms, which probably indicates a pause or change of tune, and just put it straight into Greek as *xylo*. No one can be sure. But you can imagine how the early Christians fell on that with delight as a providential translation, one of the Holy Spirit's triumphant mistakes. 'God has reigned from the tree.')

The language here is of the cross as a throne, the place from which the judgement of God is delivered, the throne of God in our midst. But Venantius also thinks of the cross as now displacing the legionary banners. Christ leads us forward, a Christian army, in our battle not against barbarians, but against the enemies of humankind. It has to be said that the later history of this hymn and its image does have its shadows. 'The royal banners' was the favourite hymn of the Crusaders, suggesting that they had somewhat missed the point of the original. Venantius was able to write about the Christian legions and the Christian army for the simple reason that there wasn't a Roman army around. For the Roman army was in disarray, retreating to the inner boundaries, receding into memory. The *vexilla* – the banners or regimental standards that he's talking about – are not the banners of another literal army. Originally, just like the triumphant victorious Lamb, this is meant to convey a creative paradox. And an even stranger image can be found a century or two after Venantius in Anglo-Saxon England, in one of the great masterpieces of Anglo-Saxon poetry, 'The Dream of the Rood' (which means 'the vision of the cross'). There Christ, 'That young champion who is God almighty', mounts the cross like a hero leaping onto his horse.

All of this rich imagery has a long and fruitful life in the Middle Ages. And it was nourished also by another expression of the victory tradition, which begins (probably) in the fourth Christian century: the tradition of the 'harrowing of hell', when Christ 'went and made proclamation to the imprisoned spirits' (1 Peter 3.19). The early

Christians wanted to know more about this, and so they imagined Christ after his death going down among the dead – going in search of those whose humanity had been imprisoned or frustrated or denied in the long history of humankind before his coming. In a fourth-century text usually called the Acts of Pilate we hear a description of what happened in the underworld on Holy Saturday. It's an eyewitness account given by the Good Thief, an intensely dramatic narrative whose main thrust is this wonderful picture of Christ pursuing his search for the lost among the spirits in prison, those captured, defeated human beings who have been raked in by the devil as his due. But they are not the devil's due; they are the property of God. The image is of a successful raid on enemy territory to free hostages and bring them home.

When I first started teaching theology about forty years ago, the image of raids to free hostages felt a little bit old-fashioned. It's a testimony to the depth at which the world still needs the redeeming cross that such an image has become contemporary once again. We know what it is now to think about the plight of hostages and prisoners. We know what it is to calculate the risks and problems of a raid to deliver them. It's no longer archaic and quaint. And it was anything but academic in the early medieval world. In art and poetry and drama, this particular way of thinking about the victory of the cross was everywhere to be found. You'll see artistic representations with the Lord carrying a pennant with the cross on it. It's the sign of his victory and he's taking it to plant it, the conqueror's flag, in the realms of death. And this incursion into the heart of enemy territory is also the dominant visual image of the resurrection among the Eastern Orthodox. For the Orthodox Christian the main icon for Easter is not an Easter morning picture, but a Holy Saturday image: Christ, very often balancing on the fallen doors, the fallen prison gates of Hell which have fallen in the shape of a cross, Christ straddling these gates, one foot on each, reaching out, grabbing Adam with his right hand and Eve with his left. And behind Adam and Eve are all the great figures of pre-Christian times waiting to be brought home – Satan's hostages being freed.

We will reflect a bit more on that Orthodox image later on in the Epilogue; but for now I'm going to end this first part of the book with just two more examples of this very rich tradition. The first is from *The Vision of Piers Plowman* – probably the greatest English theological work of the Middle Ages, except for the Revelations of Julian of Norwich. In *Piers Plowman*, a fourteenth-century writer evokes this tradition by elaborating the scene from the Acts of Pilate in an unforgettably vivid episode showing Christ descending to the dead. It begins with a quotation of Psalm 24.9: 'Lift up your heads O gates, be lifted up you everlasting doors, that the King of glory may enter.' These are the gates of the land of the dead, the gates of hell, the gates of the prison of the powers of darkness. And with a wonderful flourish the episode in *Piers Plowman* opens

> A voice loud in that light to Lucifer said
> 'Princes of this palace quickly undo the gates
> for here comes crowned the King of all glory.

Notice, 'here comes *crowned* the King of all glory': already because of the cross Jesus is crowned, already victorious. He's not hanging around for the resurrection to prove something. The incarnate crucified life is burrowing its way through the lost depths and deserts of human experience to burst out on Easter Sunday, bringing with it the lost and the dead. The same picture is found in my second example, from the great Mystery Plays of that period. My own memory is still vivid of a production of the York plays in the mid-1970s, where the lost souls wandered around on stage with a great deal of dry ice flurrying around them, with light projected onto them through a grille, like a prison window, so that all across the stage was the long shadow of a heavy black grid. And with the arrival of Christ that grid simply dropped in one dramatic moment and full unbroken light flooded in.

It's potent imagery and it led at least one great twentieth-century theologian, the Swedish bishop Gustav Aulen, to say that the real and central theology of redemption for the whole Christian world was a theology of *Christus Victor*, the victorious Christ. Aulen's book on the subject is a treasury of quotations from Christian theological history to show that this was what everybody was really talking about. It was very influential, but I have to confess that I don't think he is wholly right. We've seen, for example, how immensely important the language of sacrifice was right from the start. The New Testament is more complex than any one model. And yet Aulen does identify what is bound to be a central theme for our celebration of the cross. 'Sing my tongue the glorious battle, sing the ending of the fray.' We're drawn back to where we began: the sign, the cross as a sign of triumph. 'At the sign of triumph, Satan's legions flee.'

That sense of the cross as a sign of triumph, a sign of power and protection, also runs very deep. There's a Holy Week hymn for Compline – 'Servant of God, remember' – which concentrates on how we must, day by day and night by night, renew our baptism with the sign of the cross, because when Satan sees the mark of the cross on our foreheads he won't be able to stand it, he'll be off. And through the centuries the cult of the life-giving cross, the protecting cross, the Exaltation of the Holy Cross celebrated on 14 September, all of these (semi-legendary, sometimes even semi-superstitious) traditions draw their weight, their force, from this primary sense of the death of Christ as a victory.

As you will have gathered, the meaning of the cross of Jesus is something that constantly moves between different poles. The deeper you go into any one meaning, any one metaphor, the more it seems you're likely to bump into another one. You can't fully talk about the sign without the victory, the victory without the sacrifice. And that's as it should be. Christian theology is not a set of granite monuments that you walk around with your guidebook, ticking them off one by one as you see the great blocks of Sound Teaching. Christian theology is a more fluid, constantly moving, constantly shifting process. When you look very hard at one set of meanings they dissolve into another. And so it continues, round and round in the opposite of a vicious circle. The cross is a sign, but never just a sign because it makes a difference, whether we know it or not. The cross is a sacrifice, but a sacrifice performed by God, not by us, a sacrifice that changes our hearts. The cross is a victory, but a victory that cannot be understood except as worldly defeat. The cross, you could say, doesn't stand still. Our understanding, our absorption of its meaning, is always a living process in

> *The cross is a sign, but never just a sign because it makes a difference, whether we know it or not*

which one image, one category, again and again moves us into another.

I've quoted a number of hymns in this chapter, because it is in hymns that we learn much of our theology. (This, incidentally, makes it important to have good hymns – so that we have good theology! The average hymn book doesn't always seem to regard this as quite such a priority . . .) The best hymns begin with one set of images, and then often shift us into another. They move around, they encourage and inspire us to feel and think this and then that, and that. But many of the greatest hymns are great because they settle with one bit of the picture and just absorb it imaginatively at length. I quoted in Chapter 1 'When I survey the wondrous cross'. There is the sign of love, 'love so amazing, so divine'. But we might also point to 'O sacred head sore wounded', another 'sign'-oriented hymn, about looking and absorbing, about being wrung out and moved by what's before us. 'There is a green hill far away' is probably where most of us learned something of the language of sacrifice and substitution.

> We may not know, we cannot tell
> What pains he had to bear.
> But we believe it was for us
> He hung and suffered there.

Those superbly simple words say of course exactly what Mark and Paul and Peter say. Forget the details: just hang onto those two words: 'for us'. And then there's 'Ah, Holy Jesu, how has thou offended?' – another hymn that pushes us to reflect on what sacrifice is all about.

We all have our favourites among Passiontide hymns. But I suspect that I'm not the only one for whom 'My song is love unknown' is perhaps the finest of all the great English Passion hymns. It's a hymn that's overflowing with a wealth of biblical narrative, imagery and allusion. We have nearly everything here that we might want to say. And 'Love unknown' is a good place to end this chapter. Why 'unknown'? Surely 'My saviour's love to me' has been displayed, has been demonstrated and made known? And yet as that hymn proceeds we realize what we really don't know about the freedom of God's love. Every year as we return to reflect on it, it is the transcendence and the liberty of that love to which we are returned. And so it should be.

> Never was love, dear king.
> never was grief like thine.
> This is my friend
> in whose sweet praise
> I all my days
> might gladly spend.

We need all the images we can command and all the hymns we can sing. But as with Mrs Alexander's simple words in 'There is a green hill', or as in that immensely poignant conclusion 'This is my friend, my friend indeed', it's probably the monosyllables, the simple weighty words, that will say what we really need to say. And then, when we have said all we can say, the words of our song can be allowed to enter the depths of the way we think and live from day to day – to move us to spend our days in a praise that is service to God and to God's world, making into flesh and blood the unknown love of the God who, in the cross of Jesus, has saved us.

For reflection or discussion

1 How does it help you to know that the victory is already there in Jesus' life and in the cross?
2 Which of the early Christian or medieval images of the cross as victory speaks most to you and why?
3 Pick one of the hymns quoted in this chapter and say why it appeals to you. Does it help you to understand the cross?

Part 2

THE MEANING OF
THE RESURRECTION

4

Christ's resurrection – then

Indeed, these are not drunk, as you suppose, for it is only nine
o'clock in the morning . . . Jesus of Nazareth, a man attested
to you by God with deeds of power, wonders and signs that
God did through him among you, as you yourselves know –
this man, handed over to you according to the definite plan
and foreknowledge of God, you crucified and killed by the
hands of those outside the law. But God raised him up, having freed him from death, because it was impossible for him
to be held in its power.   (Acts 2.15, 22b–24, NRSV)

In this chapter I want to reflect on the resurrection of Jesus
Christ as it's represented and reflected on in the New Testament, on what it meant for people in the first century to
say they believed Jesus had risen from the dead. This will
take us to some thoughts about the historical foundation
of resurrection belief; but I'll begin with the question of
what the claim that Jesus is risen from the dead meant
back then, at the beginning of the New Testament era.

The end has begun

I'm going to explore four aspects of this; and I begin with
Acts 2 and Peter's sermon on the day of Pentecost. Whether

or not this is exactly what Peter said on the day of Pentecost, we don't know. Probably not; writers of the time were happy to put together from tradition and educated guessing the sort of thing that someone should have said on such and such an occasion, and their readers would have understood that this was part of how the story should be told. So, as many scholars have suggested, what we're dealing with here must represent a very early stratum of Christian preaching. This is the *sort* of thing, at the very least, that people were saying. And it's particularly striking that Peter begins (2.17) with a quotation from the prophecy of Joel, about the last days: 'In the last days, God says, I will pour out my Spirit on all people.' If you're wondering why the apostles are behaving so strangely on Pentecost, it's because the last days have arrived, the end of the world is at the door. And how and why have they arrived? Because of the life and death and resurrection of Jesus.

There is our theological starting point. Believing in the resurrection is believing that the new age has been inaugurated, the new world has begun. And that new world is, as we might put it, the final phase of the history of God's relation with his people. So to say 'Jesus is risen' is to say that we have now entered on the last days, on the final, decisive phase of God's interaction with Israel and, through Israel, with the whole world.

Those of you who know Tom Wright's wonderful book *The Resurrection of the Son of God* will know how very clearly he's spelled out the mistakes people have sometimes made in reading New Testament texts about the 'last days' or the 'end times'. The end of the world, for people in Jesus' day, didn't mean quite what placard-wearing people on street corners might now mean by it, nor indeed what a great many American fundamentalists seem to mean by it. The end of the world meant for the people of that age that God was establishing this final phase of his action; God had brought in a new age, but a new age that was still historical and earthly. It opened out onto eternity, but it represented in itself a great transition from the old to the new.

And so if the resurrection of Jesus means that the last days have begun, this also means that after the resurrection there's never going to be any new framework, any different way of seeing God in the world. This is it. God and the world are now, you might say, settled in the full and final shape of their relationship. The decisive difference has been made. The end has begun. The kingdom has come. Jesus has advanced out of mere history into

> The end has begun. The kingdom has come. Jesus has advanced out of mere history into God's future

God's future. Jesus inhabits God's future fully, so that we who are drawn to be with Jesus in his resurrection are there with him in the future which has already been inaugurated. And that in turn opens out onto the perspective that Paul mentions more than once, of how the gift of the Holy Spirit is the foretaste or down-payment of God's future, the age to come.

And so, since this is the beginning of the last phase of human history, since the resurrection of Jesus has made the decisive difference, there's also a sense in which the destinies of all human beings are now bound up with Jesus. From now on, all human beings will find who they are, who they may be, where they will be, in relation to the figure of Jesus. The future is in his hands and his resurrection gives him that authority. It's described very clearly in Acts 17 in Paul's sermon in Athens: 'He has set a day when he will judge the world with justice by the man he has appointed. He has given proof of this to all by raising him from the dead' (v. 31). Once again, the future, the judgement, God's decisive fixing of his relationship with the world is all connected with Jesus and with Jesus' resurrection.

So this is what I believe to be the starting point in understanding belief about the resurrection in the pages of the New Testament. It is a belief that history has changed and that we are in the new phase.

Jesus without limits

As I have already indicated (and here's my second point), in this new and final phase of human history there is one and only one ultimate authority in the universe that we know: and that is Jesus. He has been set free from all that holds back the growth of humanity towards God. He has been set free from the consequences of sin in the world, from the corruption, the downward spiral, of human history. He has been set free from death. He is alive, and there is nothing now that limits his action, his liberty. 'Christ, once raised from the dead, is never going to die again,' says St Paul in Romans 6.9. And likewise in 1 Corinthians 15 we see how the resurrection is connected with that freedom and authority of Jesus: all things are given into his hands (1 Corinthians 15.24–28; cf John 16.15).

To believe in the resurrection, then, is to believe that Jesus, in the great phrase of John Masefield, is 'alive and at large in the world'; Jesus is set free, he's not going to die again, nothing prevents him acting, he is always going to be active and not passive, always at work. And so, to say he is risen is to say he is now free to *act* eternally, unceasingly, without limit. Death and its effects cannot hold him back. It's not only, then, that we are brought into the new age, brought into this final phase of human history. That final phase is shaped, controlled by the liberty of Jesus. To say he is risen is to say he is free to act. Wherever we are now in human history after the resurrection Jesus is active.

The bridge between God and humanity

And so to my third point. The new age has begun, and Jesus is now free to act universally, eternally and without limit; but *who* is it that acts eternally, universally and without limit? The answer, of course, is God. And so in this new age, this final phase of human history, the action of God is bound up with the action of Jesus. What Jesus is doing is what God is doing. If Jesus is free to act wherever he wants, to be wherever he wants, to be with whoever he wants, then his action carries in it the freedom of God himself, that freedom from death and limit, from the downward spiral of human sin and failure. Jesus is free to act for God and in God, and God in him. In the new age you can't disentangle what Jesus is doing from what God is doing.

This means that, from now on, Jesus is in the position of what the New Testament calls a mediator. He stands as a bridge between God and humanity: not keeping them apart, but bringing them together. He is, in the language most associated with the letter to the Hebrews, the Priest who alone passes backwards and forwards between the inner mysteries of God, the inmost sanctuary, and the world of human interaction. And more than that, Jesus brings us to be where he is. Wherever he wills to be in the world, he is always, in the language of John's Gospel (1.18), 'in the bosom of the Father', next to the Father's heart, 'in the closest relationship with the Father'. At the same time his freedom opens up for us a place to stand in relation to God and the world. We move into the space that Jesus has cleared for us: the new and living way that's opened up to us the Holy Place where God dwells. Jesus has created for us a space that we can occupy, in his name.

In other words, Jesus' resurrection has made it possible for us to live where he lives. And of course if you occupy the same space, you can say you share the same embodiment. So we who have been drawn into the community created by Jesus can call ourselves the *body* of Christ. We occupy Jesus' identity in the world and before God. We are where Jesus 'happens' in the world and before God. He has gone to prepare a place for us, as John's Gospel puts it (14.2). So not only is he acting for God and in God; this action for God and in God makes space for us to live in God's presence and to live for God and the world. We come to embody the new age, living in the Lord of the new age who has the freedom to act for God and to bring us to be where he is in relation to God.

Jesus and God are one

That brings me to my fourth point. After the resurrection God himself comes to be defined in relation to Jesus. He is the God who raised Jesus from the dead, a phrase that recurs many times in the letters of Paul. What God is it we're talking about? *That* God. The fact that God has raised Jesus becomes the identifying characteristic of God. So, just as you can't really disentangle the action of Jesus from the action of God, so you can't now disentangle the identity of God from the identity of Jesus. The resurrection tells us, again as the New Testament puts it, that God has refused and overturned the verdict of the world on Jesus. The world, in the shape of the political

The resurrection tells us that God has refused and overturned the verdict of the world on Jesus

and religious authorities, has said no to Jesus, and God has said no to that no. In other words, God has said yes to Jesus. He has endorsed all that Jesus is, does and says.

God has put his stamp of authority on Jesus, defining what Jesus does and says and gives as what God does and says and gives. What Jesus does is what God does and what God does is what Jesus does. The God we're talking about is the God who said yes to Jesus by raising him from the dead: that is the Christian God.

The resurrection and the Church

Those four aspects of the resurrection that I've just outlined are actually very widely spread throughout the New Testament. You don't need to take one or two isolated texts: these are themes that run right through the letters of St Paul, and they're there in Hebrews, John, Acts and elsewhere. And at the heart of all these aspects of Christ's resurrection is that bewildering realization from which they all unfold: that we're now living in a new phase of history, which is the final and decisive phase of God's relationship with the world he's made.

All that we have seen so far suggests that the leading themes of Christian doctrine have their root in the claim that Jesus is raised from the dead. This is where Christology – doctrine (or teaching) about Christ – begins. What you say about Jesus is now determined by all these aspects of the risen Jesus. You can't simply have a theology about Jesus which is about the Jesus who walked in Galilee and nothing more. Now, because of the resurrection, you have a stimulus and opportunity, indeed an imperative, to think more fully and more deeply about Jesus, because the Jesus whose resurrection has inaugurated the new age, who is alive and at large wherever he wants to be in this new context, is a Jesus who can't just be contained in the terms of a merely human biography.

That is why Christianity is not the Jesus of Nazareth Society – rather like the Alfred Lord Tennyson Society or some such thing, looking back to a great dead genius. The Church was never that and (please God) never will be. Whenever we find ourselves drifting into that mode of thinking or feeling, we have cause to worry. But if the resurrection is the basis of our thinking about Jesus, then it's the basis of our new thinking about God, and it's the basis of the doctrine of God as Trinity. God acts fully and freely in Jesus his Son, and one dimension of that full and free action of God in Jesus is the giving of that life-giving breath that makes us alive in a new way – otherwise known as the Holy Spirit. So as our thinking about the resurrection unfolds, we see how we move towards speaking of God as Father and Son and Holy Spirit. The resurrection is the seed of the whole theology of Christian orthodoxy: and it's also the seed of the theology of the Church. Belief in the resurrection is what makes the Church more than just the Jesus of Nazareth Society. Because, believing in the resurrection and the new creation, the new age, the final phase of God's action, means that those who relate to Jesus, relate to him as a contemporary, not as a memory, as a reality over against them, not just in their heads and thoughts,

> *Belief in the resurrection is what makes the Church more than just the Jesus of Nazareth Society*

are being drawn to stand with Jesus in his present life, the life he now lives to God. And that's why the Church speaks of Jesus as 'God with us' – alive and active in all that we say and do in response to his presence with us through the Spirit.

Think of those typical identifying actions of the Church: the reading of the Bible; the proclamation of the Gospel; the baptizing of people; the sharing of bread and wine in Holy Communion. None of these would begin to make sense unless we believed that Jesus was contemporary. We might read the Bible in other terms. If Jesus were not alive and contemporary we would read it as an historical document, we wouldn't read it listening for a word which would create a present encounter. We might have initiation ceremonies – plenty of people do – but we wouldn't have an initiation ceremony that claimed we were somehow entering into, here and now, the abiding reality of a Jesus crucified and raised from the dead, or receiving life-giving breath from him – the Holy Spirit.

And we might have a memorial meal, a commemoration feast like Oxbridge colleges, but we wouldn't, I think, see it as the partaking, here and now, of a life that makes us alive. That's why a theology of the Church takes for granted the resurrection, and why if you don't have a vital belief in the resurrection you lose your theology of the Church. That's just a little bit of an indication of how these interweaving themes about the freedom and authority of Jesus, the interweaving of Jesus' action and God's action through the resurrection, start off the process of thinking, praying and reflecting that finally bear fruit in the Christian creeds and sacraments.

The resurrection and history

In the rest of this chapter I want to turn to a second question: how did it actually start? Where is the historical core of all this? I won't go into the great plethora of scholarly debate that's been around this in the last hundred years or so. But there are one or two things which I think need saying in relation to that.

Despite every effort, it's proved extremely difficult to identify in the New Testament any stratum of tradition or belief that doesn't have the resurrection at its heart – just as we have seen in earlier chapters how difficult it is to find a stratum of biblical writing that doesn't take the cross for granted. There have been some who have tried: those who've reconstructed the supposed document that lies behind Matthew and Luke – the 'Q' document of Jesus' sayings – have sometimes argued that there must have been a primitive Christian document of some sort which simply listed the sayings of Jesus and had no theology of the cross or the resurrection. This ambitious theory has been shipwrecked several times over on the unhappy fact (in the judgement of most scholars) that the very earliest and most impeccable layers of tradition in the Gospel include Jesus' invitation to take up his cross and follow him, and include an obstinately irreducible number of reflections on the Passion and the resurrection.

We can't, it seems, get behind this. It's not as if somewhere there is a straightforward pre-resurrection form of Christianity that allows us to think that Jesus was a very nice person, and lets us off the hook in other ways. It can't be excavated. No faith, in the New Testament, seems to be definable or identifiable independently of the resurrection. Even if you look at those documents like the letter of James and the letter to the Hebrews, where the language of resurrection is not obviously around, the references to the lordship and the glory of Jesus, the joy of Jesus, the entry of Jesus into heaven, presuppose that something has happened and something has changed. And it seems there's good ground (given the rest of the New Testament) for calling it the resurrection unless we can think of something better.

The Christian community exists, in New Testament terms, because of the conviction that a new age has begun, that something decisive has happened and a change has been made. And so it's very hard to see how that new age faith – faith in and because of the resurrection – could come into being without an event that people could point to: an event, not just a transaction in people's minds. Again, there have been some very interesting, subtle and complex suggestions

> *The Christian community exists, in New Testament terms, because of the conviction that a new age has begun*

about how the belief in Jesus' resurrection might have evolved over a longish period; as the believing community reflected on the sayings and actions of Jesus and on the meaning of his execution, gradually there came into focus a conviction that he was, in some way, alive. (Those of you who've seen that brilliant and challenging film *Jesus of Montreal* will recognize that story.) And this, in itself, would be quite an interesting and compelling story; but it's not the story that any element of the New Testament puts before us, and you have to suspend a great deal of disbelief in order to suppose that this, rather than what we actually have in the New Testament, is primitive and prior.

One of my academic colleagues in years gone by used say with some exasperation that there were theologies of the resurrection that really amounted to not much more than saying that at some point on Easter Sunday or soon after, something in Peter's mind suddenly went 'ping'! His point was that in the first century people didn't think like that. Events were events and what happened in your mind, your attitude, wasn't an event in quite the same sense as is being taken for granted here. That whole conviction – that God had turned the verdict of the world upside down, had said no to the no that the world was saying – would for a first-century Jew have meant very clearly a belief that something had happened which *embodied* the new, divine verdict: something not just in the minds of human beings, but beyond them.

It's also worth bearing in mind that when Jewish people in Jesus' era talked about resurrection, they really meant what they said: they meant the dead being raised to earth rather than to heaven. When, in the book of Daniel, we read the prophecy about those who will be raised from the dust in the last days, it's pretty clear that what Daniel had in mind was people returning to this earth. And nobody has yet been able to find a form of Jewish belief in the resurrection that allowed very much ambiguity on that. This language of resurrection is historical, not speculative: it's about earth before it's about heaven. And a belief in resurrection that did not involve that standing again upon the earth would have been very alien to people in the first Christian century.

All of this makes me extremely suspicious of accounts of the resurrection that simply make it internal to the minds of Christian believers. As we see it in the New Testament, it is something that *came* to the apostles, not something on which they stumbled as they thought about it. That, I think, is what the New Testament puts before us, and one may or may not believe the New Testament's claim; but I think it's important to understand that that is what's being claimed.

As we reflect on what's being claimed, whether or not we want to subscribe to it, it is worth pausing and noting some features of the way in which the resurrection stories are told.

If the *Jesus of Montreal* kind of story were true, I would expect the texts deriving from that story to be very polished, carefully crafted products: the result of a long period of reflection, using literary allusions and weaving together a complicated picture. Yet what we have is a series of resurrection stories that are abrupt, confused, vivid and unpolished. I don't think one can overemphasize that oddity about the resurrection stories. It was once fashionable to sneer at the fact that there are four not-easily-compatible versions of what happened on Easter Sunday and afterwards: as if that were a sign of their untruth. But when you think a bit more about it, the very untidiness of the resurrection stories is one of the main reasons for taking them seriously as historical reportage. What's going on is clearly people struggling to find words for something they had not expected.

This comes over most clearly in a very interesting way, which I don't think has been discussed all that much in the literature. Read Mark's Gospel and you will read a long, involved and slightly ritualized account of the Passion of Jesus: a story much polished in the telling – a story which, some scholars say, probably has its origins in disciples literally 'walking the way of the cross' around Jerusalem. You'll notice how place after place is identified, as if you're being given a kind of route map of Jerusalem. In each place, allusions are made to prophecies in the Old Testament. This is a story that has drawn into itself the whole penumbra of allusions, echoes, people recognizing patterns, sayings, metaphors, images from the Old Testament. Even the little incident of the young man running away naked from the Garden of Gethsemane resonates with a line in the prophecy of Amos: 'the strong in heart shall flee away naked on that day' (2.16). This is not to say that these details are unhistorical. But they are thought through: 'as the Scriptures say', 'as it is written', 'as it was prophesied'.

But then Mark turns to the resurrection, giving his account in those abrupt, extraordinary sentences in the last chapter of his Gospel, as if it's still fresh and as if nobody has quite told the story before. Something happened that left people dumbstruck. Think of the famous short ending of Mark – 'They said nothing to anybody because they were afraid' – where we are left in mid-air. Even in literary style, the abruptness is very clear: *ephobounto gar* in the Greek (16.8), 'they were afraid, you see'. It's a very odd way of ending a book. Ever since, people have been wondering what was going on. But, likewise, even in the much more elaborated stories of the resurrection appearances in Matthew, Luke and John, what's missing is that self-conscious literary element that we find in the

Passion stories. You don't have clear allusions to the Old Testament, you don't have literary models on which people are working. You have stories that seem to be squeezed, forced into being by the sheer pressure of events.

There have been studies by distinguished scholars that have sought to argue for literary analogues to the resurrection stories in some Old Testament tales: yet for all the immense learning that has gone into such argument, at the end of the day we are left with a small handful of possible echoes. Again and again, people have come up against a brick wall on this issue. Whereas elsewhere in the Gospels (in the nativity stories, in parts of the body of the story of Jesus' ministry, in the story of the Passion) people are aware somehow of fulfilment, balance, echo and pattern, so that they use the Old Testament freely to interpret the tradition of what happened, where the resurrection stories are in question you don't have that: it's as if the fact of the new age, the new phase of history, has created a new form of storytelling, as if you had to make up your way of telling this story because there were no precedents, because quite literally nothing like this had ever happened. And that, of course, despite the statements by Paul and others that Christ was raised from the dead 'according to the Scriptures'. There is strikingly little elaboration of this alleged fulfilment of Scripture. Even granted that sense that in some way this is a fulfilment of earlier Scripture, nonetheless, when it comes to it, the story doesn't fit neatly into any pre-existing pattern.

This is one of the decisive things that ought to make us take the Gospel accounts of the resurrection with absolute seriousness, as pressed into existence by facts – not literary meditations, not people ten years later trying to make sense of an experience on which they have been reflecting. There is, it has been said, a quality of 'rawness' about these stories, and a quality of mysteriousness: there is the strange but very persistent theme that people do not at first recognize the risen Jesus – the story of the encounter with Mary Magdalene, the story of Emmaus. That is a significant factor once again which no one has ever fully made sense of, and again doesn't fit easily into literary stereotypes. There are cases in the Old Testament when people realize belatedly that they have been talking to an angel, when the angel suddenly reveals his glory; but that's not quite how it works in the encounter with Mary Magdalene or the Emmaus story. And so, in thinking about the historical basis of the resurrection stories, about the empty tomb and the 'apparitions', it is important to be alert to the way the story is told and to begin to see how much of a shock it actually was – and, of course, still is.

The story is told in a new way because nothing like this has ever happened before; and we are still finding it difficult because nothing like that has ever happened again.

But (to go right back to where I began) that is what you might expect in retrospect; what you might expect if what you're dealing with is an event that inaugurates a new phase in human history, not just another episode in the continuing story, but something that reshapes the whole way in which we talk about God, and about God's world.

Now there are many points of detail about the resurrection stories – about the way in which the empty tomb is spoken of, about the content and the direction of some of the apparition stories (not least the apparition to Thomas or the apparition to Peter and the Beloved Disciple by the Sea of Galilee at the end of John's Gospel) – on which it would be fascinating to spend more time. But I hope that the main point is clear. There is something about the way in which these stories are told that continues to stand out: a change of gear between the Passion and the resurrection story – a sense of the new.

To claim then that Jesus is 'risen indeed' is to claim that we are never going to be able to speak completely adequately about Jesus as risen; we are in this sense out of our depth. And that is quite a good place to be in gospel terms. When Jesus encourages his disciples to 'Put out into deep water' (Luke 5.4), that's not just a word for the first century but a word for now.

The writers of the New Testament are struggling to find a way of speaking adequately concerning something for which there is no precedent, struggling to find a way of making real – for the reader and the hearer – a mystery. Not a mystery in the sense of something that is obscure, something deserving to be clarified; but a mystery in the sense of something too big to be contained. We are, in

The writers of the New Testament are struggling to find a way of speaking adequately concerning something for which there is no precedent

this context, very much the ant crawling round the foot of the elephant trying to work out what exactly is going on in this enormous reality up above. And even the most eloquent and exciting passages in the New Testament about the resurrection – like 1 Corinthians 15 – still have about them that sense of being out of one's depth.

So, to conclude this chapter, I am suggesting that to understand how the resurrection works in the New Testament we have to understand the claim that is being made – of the inauguration of the last phase of God's action in the world's history – and to see that as bound to an event that has changed the frame of reference for ever. Getting that event in clear focus is almost impossible. We have a tumult of different voices about what happened on the first Easter day, all of them reflecting just that confusion and unclarity that are the marks of people speaking about life-changing experiences and unique moments.

We can't set up the hidden video camera in the garden on Easter eve and find out what really happened. What we have instead is the impact of an event that caused people to believe that the world had changed for ever, and that Jesus did not belong to the past. I believe that this was an event that resulted in the tomb being empty, and in Jesus actually appearing to his friends – but whatever the exact nature of the event, it had the power to produce the belief that the world had changed for ever: that this particular human being, Jesus, not only didn't belong to the past, but was from now on bound up in how we talk about God, so that anything that is ever said about God again must have some reference to Jesus.

For reflection or discussion

1 How does believing you are living in the last phase of human history help your understanding of Jesus and his risen life?

2 Have you ever tended to view the Church as no more than the Jesus of Nazareth Society? How does the idea of Jesus as 'God with us' help to dispel this view?

3 What is claimed about the historical basis of the resurrection stories and why? Do you subscribe to it? Why or why not?

5

Christ's resurrection – now

If Christ has not been raised, your faith is futile and you are still in your sins. Then those also who have died in Christ have perished. If for this life only we have hoped in Christ, we are of all people most to be pitied.

But in fact Christ has been raised from the dead, the first fruits of those who have died. For since death came through a human being, the resurrection of the dead has also come through a human being; for as all die in Adam, so all will be made alive in Christ. But each in his own order: Christ the first fruits, then at his coming those who belong to Christ. Then comes the end, when he hands over the kingdom to God the Father, after he has destroyed every ruler and every authority and power. For he must reign until he has put all his enemies under his feet. The last enemy to be destroyed is death.

(1 Corinthians 15.17–26, NRSV)

In this final chapter I want to look at five broad areas where I think the preaching of the resurrection of Jesus Christ today has a direct impact on our lives, on what we want to communicate to people around us, and to the world in general: five dimensions of the good news that are rooted in the resurrection.

Human beings matter

First: to believe that Jesus is risen is to believe that when you've worked it all out, Jesus is the point where human histories converge. But that implies, of course, that there is such a thing as a human being. To say humanity exists, that there is such a thing as a human being, is to say there is something about being human that is non-negotiable: we are human because God has created us like this and we are human because God has destined us for communion with him through Jesus Christ, and whatever human being you meet in any situation whatsoever, there is something absolutely central, non-negotiable, about that. There is such a thing as humanity. Because Jesus is Lord, and if all human stories converge on him – if he is, as Browning said in his wonderful poem on the fourth Gospel ('A Death in the Desert'), 'the groom to every bride', the one who completes every human life – then there is such a thing as humanity. And that means we have grounds for resisting all those things that get in the way of humanity: all those ways, subtle and unsubtle, that human beings have invented to stop themselves and other people from being human beings.

If Jesus is risen, there is a human destiny

So we begin with that pronouncement, that if Jesus is risen, there is a human destiny. Every human life

84

has something about it, distinctive, given by God, given in the hope of Christ. And I've always been very taken by those theologians, especially in the Eastern Christian world, who've emphasized that human beings were made with dignity and liberty so that, one day, they would be companions for Jesus Christ. Human nature was endowed with all its gifts so that it would one day be a proper vehicle for the transforming work of God the Father.

So without underrating the capacity of human beings for destructiveness and for reducing their world to chaos and pain, the resurrection imposes on us a very high doctrine of humanity. It tells us not only that God exists but that *we* do, and that we have a purpose and a destiny. And if it's true that the resurrection tells us there's never going to be any change in the frame of reference in which God relates to us, that's the kind of conviction that leads people to resist so bravely when they're up against inhuman systems. The people who resist dehumanizing tyrannies, in our age or in any age, are on the whole people who believe not only in God but in humanity – not just in humanity in a sort of humanistic and optimistic sense but humanity as having its dignity and its glory grounded in communion with God in Jesus Christ.

So there's a first dimension of good news: if Jesus is risen, human beings really exist, and they exist for a purpose. And there's something about them that can't be taken away by tyranny or convenience, by the hard totalitarianisms that we've seen so much of in the twentieth century, or by the soft totalitarianism that erodes our sense of what's humanly distinctive in a more comfortable culture. And that also says something about how we approach the Bible. It may sound a slightly odd connection to make, but bear with me for a moment. If human beings really exist and they find their destiny in relation to Jesus, then there is something about that book which conveys to us the reality of Jesus that remains resonant for all kinds of human being. There's something about that book that is fundamentally human as well as divine. And human beings as they read it may expect to find themselves addressed in the depth of their humanity, challenged and enriched.

That's a sort of footnote to what I've been saying about human nature at large. It means that wherever we go, with the biblical story in our hands and with the vision of Jesus in our eyes, there is an expectation that human beings will resonate with what's being spoken of. They may not quite know how they do it or why, and they may not do it in the ways or at the times or in the contexts where we'd like them to. But we go on in mission, because of that conviction that there is such a thing as the human heart and human destiny, and thus that these words will find an echo.

This should excite us: Christians read the Bible not as a document from history but as a world into which they enter so that God may meet them. That's what the Bible's there for, and this only makes sense in the light of a resurrection belief. I've argued once or twice in the past that the whole doctrine of Christ's Lordship develops and fleshes itself out in the early Church in the very process of mission. You understand more fully who Jesus is the more people you try and share him with. Because people recognize him, though they come from wildly diverse backgrounds; they recognize him, though their humanity is very diverse; they recognize the humanity they share with him and so open up their own humanity to God. Something similar may apply to how we use the Bible. It does still amaze me (and I speak as no fundamentalist) that the Bible continues to be a book that decisively, critically illuminates the humanity of people from such wildly diverse cultural backgrounds. And whatever the challenges there are about interpreting it in those various backgrounds, it's still that story, those words, which have that effect. And this is unmistakeably connected with the resurrection affirmation that Jesus is forever active in the world.

The world has changed

So, moving on to the second dimension of good news: the world really can change. If the resurrection is about an all-important, decisive, central moment around which the whole history of the world pivots and turns in a new direction, something has happened within history that has altered what is possible. Someone has made an irreversible breakthrough in the definition of humanity which can never be undone. To believe that the world can change, that God can turn history on its pivot, is to believe

> *Something has happened within history that has altered what is possible*

that in all sorts of human situations it is possible for things to be different. And I think that's the basis of all the ways in which Christians are regularly and systematically a nuisance to people who want a tidy world. The Roman Empire was, in many ways, a very efficient and comprehensive and well-run organization. Unfortunately, it didn't have room for the vision of humanity that the gospel introduced. And thus Christianity was a nuisance to the Roman Empire, as it was a nuisance to the Third Reich and the Soviet Union. It's quite a challenge in contemporary China. It even has its nuisance moments in the UK and the USA . . . And it's because of this conviction that the way things happen to be is not the way they have to be that Christians go on being tiresome, saying, 'It *could* be that human beings could live into a bigger space, a higher vocation, a greater glory.'

One of the wonderful things that Christianity always says to human beings in absolutely any situation is, 'There's more to you than you think.' That's not to buy into the awful modern sentimentality of saying, 'You can be anything you want to be.' It does say, 'The way things are is not the way things are destined to be. Under God, with wisdom, discernment and courage, you can find out what changes are possible, because the world *can* change.' God *can* be known and served: human beings *can* live differently: the body of Christ shows us there are ways of living together as human beings that are not tribal, violent, exclusive and anxious. That's quite a bit of good news to be going on with. It's what St Paul talks about when he writes in Galatians 6 about life in the Spirit. It's about that counter-cultural reality which says to the world around, 'It doesn't have to be like this, there's more to it than that.' It's living at odds with the world's systems of rivalries, the world's systems of mutual exclusion and fear. And all of that is about living really, truly and fully in God's future, beginning now. God can rule now, already, the kingdom has drawn near, is at hand, round the corner, on the doorstep.

St Augustine, in his great treatise on the City of God, said that the kingdom of God was, in effect, the lives of the saints. Holy people show what it's like for God to rule. This may be an illuminating way of thinking about the saints, that they're where the kingdom of God is; and you can name your own saints – not just the ones in the windows or the calendar, but the people you know who have shown the kingdom, the possibility of things being different. There is such a thing as humanity. Human history can change. God can rule here and now.

Death cannot defeat us

But it's not just about here and now, and here's the third dimension of good news. In the sort of perspective we've been outlining, death is real and yet conquerable. You don't have to deny the reality of death: in fact there couldn't be anything worse than denying the reality of death, because that is encouraging people to live out a lie. What you can say is that God is never at the end of his resources when we are at the end of ours. When we face death, God says, 'I'm on the far side of it', and a relationship with God is therefore not exhausted by the set of horizons we're used to here and now. Such a relationship is what is meant by eternal life – not just life after death and not just some sort of survival of death. Christians really ought to be much more critical than they often are of the idea that we survive death. We don't. We die, and God brings us to life as he restores our relationship with him. That, I believe, is the biblical proclamation; it's not that some little bit of us somehow hangs on rather half-heartedly for some indefinite period, but that God remakes us. And that is one of the things that enables us to face, honestly, our fear of death and annihilation.

I've sometimes said that our belief in eternal life and resurrection life with God in heaven doesn't depend so much on what we believe about our humanity, as if there were a little immortal bit of it that hangs on: it depends on what we believe about *God*, that God is the God who raised Jesus from the dead, the God who raises the dead, the God who brings what is from what is not, who brings life out of death. So that's the third aspect: not a bland proclamation that we can hope for immortality in the general sense of surviving things, but the ability to confront death and the utter reality

Our horizons, bounded by death, are not God's horizons

of the loss and the tragedy involved, knowing that God is greater, and that our horizons, bounded by death, are not God's horizons. And when we've learned to look death in the face, then all kind of other fears and anxieties fall into perspective.

In addressing our fear of death, the good news addresses so many other fears as well, because so many of our fears are actually variants of the fear of death – the fear of defeat, annihilation, powerlessness, the fear of not being there, not being able to make our presence felt or make our will real. And God through the resurrection says to each one of us – as of course Jesus says so often, so firmly in the Gospels – do not be afraid. It is so telling that the words of Jesus after the resurrection to his disciples are, again and again, 'Don't be afraid!' Or elsewhere, 'I have over-come the world' or 'It is I.' And when the very roots of our anxiety and fear are challenged in that way, this is part of the process by which we come to be less afraid of one another, of what's different or uncomfortable. When we face what's really other – the person, or situation, culture, philosophy, religion – quite often the anxiety with which we approach it is an anxiety that perhaps we won't survive the encounter. But if God has said to us, 'Don't be afraid, I have overcome the world,' what exactly is there to be afraid of? It's a major theme to take on board, but the funda-mental fearlessness that ought to come if we really heard the gospel of the resurrection will begin to affect and dissolve so many other of our fears. It's this absolute sense of rooted-ness in what God has done which pervades the letters of Paul. It's to do with the confidence that we have that a place has been cleared for us, a place to stand, a place where we belong with Jesus in the presence of God the Father.

Christ prays within us

The fourth dimension of the good news which the resur-rection has to tell us about is quite a practical one – about our prayer. I think all I've said so far really obliges us to think quite hard and quite freshly about prayer. It's far too easy to fall into the way of thinking of prayer as a sort of 'storming' of heaven, a campaign: somehow we've got to get enough petitions together to make God change his mind; or we've really got to exert a bit of pressure on God to make him do what we want; or even, God's a very long way off and we've got to make a lot of noise to attract his attention; and all the various other distortions of prayer that are around. But if we are being introduced into a new world, the place where Jesus is, then prayer is most deeply 'allowing God to happen in us', the Spirit bringing Christ alive in us, being in the place where Christ is real, with the Spirit coming into us to bring Christ alive in our own hearts.

This is very much what St Paul writes on virtually every page, especially of the Corinthian letters. We enter in the Spirit, into the place of the risen Christ, saying, 'Abba, Father'. We let Christ literally 'take place' in us, happen, live in us. And that is one of the roots of silent and contemplative prayer, where in suspending our own concerns, words and fussiness we let God be in us. We breathe in, deeply, taking the Holy Spirit into body, mind and soul, so that Christ may breathe out. Breathe out, and the words 'Abba, Father' say what he has to say, eternally, to God the Father. The practice of silent prayer rests on the resurrection mystery, that Christ has made a place for us: we could not make very much sense of the distinctively Christian understanding of contemplation without that resurrection dimension. There are, of course, plenty of techniques and traditions in the religions of the world that value contemplation or meditation in silence, and from many of them we can learn (and I have learned a huge amount from them myself). But for us to make something like *Christian* sense of it all, we need that Trinitarian perspective, grounded in the resurrection. When I come before God in silence, I come before God allowing the Holy Spirit to put Christ's words into my mouth, to let my breath be breathed anew by the Spirit, carrying the words of Christ, and just let the Trinity be where I am when I pray.

We could not make sense of such a practice without belief in the resurrection, without the belief that Christ, having passed from death to life, belongs now in God's eternity. As one French theologian put it, 'Jesus is tipped over into the eternal life of God.' Standing eternally before God: holding our place there before God, so that where he is there we may be also (John 12.26). Prayer does not have to be an attempt to get God's attention, not an action we perform on God all the time, but the action God desires to perform in us to bring us to life. And when people are faced with deep anxieties about their prayer life, it can at times be of the greatest importance to say to them, 'Prayer is also letting God be God.' And if you're feeling that you're exhausting yourself with the endless effort to concentrate properly, to get from here to there (wherever 'there' is) you may very well need to hear the good news that prayer is also God being God in you, if you let him. It's not simple, or without hard work, because letting God be God in you requires you to do a fair amount of spring-cleaning en route. But that's perhaps for another day. The good news is that prayer is given

> *Prayer is not something we squeeze out with effort, but something that happens when we let God be God*

to us as well as achieved, that prayer is not something we squeeze out with effort, but something that happens when we let God be God.

God cares for all creation

And then, fifth: our worship is about God coming to be in our midst, but also about God coming to deal with the *wholeness* of who we are. The resurrection of the body means, at least in part, that all that we are is of interest to God. And so to proclaim the resurrection is to say, 'God's purpose is the transfiguration, not the cancellation, of history in the material world.' God does not want to rub out what's there so that he can do something better, God is interested in all that we have become as historical and material beings, and that's what he will raise up. Which, of course, gives a very serious and very profound theological valuation not just to our bodily and material selves, but to the material world in which we live. Belief in the resurrection has something very significantly to do

95

with how we look at our environment. And part of the good news that Christians have to utter and express in a world very anxious about that material environment is that the matter of this world is *God's before it is ours*: that it requires our respect because God sees the whole of creation and thinks it good. And thus the affirmation of Jesus' resurrection, the great decisive change in the middle of material history, bears on how we see the material world as a whole. It touches our thoughts about the environment: it bears on climate change and energy usage and carbon footprints and all the rest, which may seem a very long way from Acts 2, and yet is not so far when you think it through. It grounds also the understanding of the Church's worship as sacramental – sacramental life which is not just a sort of magical attitude to things, but the belief that the material things of this world – water and bread and wine – can become precious carriers of the purpose and work of God when they're brought into relation with the risen Jesus.

The importance, in our eucharistic liturgy, of calling the Holy Spirit down upon *ourselves* and upon these material things is that we are actually asking in our eucharistic prayer for God to do something 'resurrection-shaped' in the middle of our worship, for him to bring himself to life, as the bread is broken and the wine is shared and as we stretch out our hands and open our mouths. Without going into the immensely complicated details of the history of controversies over the presence of Christ in the Eucharist, I would want to say there are two absolutely basic things about Christ's presence in Holy Communion that we need to hold fast to. One is that it is the action of God; the second is that God shows what he means in the things of this world. This is what it is for a resurrection-shaped event to be going on in Holy Communion. So the resurrection tells us something about how God sees history and matter, the stuff of our ordinary experience; how God is free to transfigure it in relation to Jesus; and how that transfigures our own understanding of our bodies and the environment in which we live, giving us very good reasons for being very suspicious of any Christianity that ignores the value of the body and that ignores the value of the environment – and yet looking not just for affirmation but also for transformation.

And all of this reminds us that the purposes and meanings of God are not just about what goes on in our heads, but about what we do with our bodies. The ethics of both sex and economics are grounded here. What we do with our bodies matters, speaks, communicates. What we do with our possessions matters, speaks, communicates. And that's why the resurrection has a decisive impact on how we think through moral questions. Christian morality is never just 'rule-keeping', it's always about how our selves, our souls and bodies become signs of who and what God is:

signs of faithfulness, generosity, grace and mercy. When my beloved and respected former colleague Oliver O'Donovan wrote his first major book many years ago, he entitled it *Resurrection and Moral Order*: it is a long, persuasive and very sophisticated argument to say that belief in the resurrection is the foundation of all ethics. I think the Paul of 1 Corinthians would have understood that very well.

We have been thinking about the resurrection and what it means today, and we've seen that it's not simply to be seen as an isolated miracle of the past which confirms Jesus' authority, though that is part of it. We've seen that the resurrection is also a present reality, a reality that orders and organizes our life together as Christians, life in the body of Christ. The resurrection is what prompts into existence that new language that Christians speak, in their words and in their actions. The resurrection is the ground of how we make sense in what we do as much as in what we say.

> The resurrection is what prompts into existence that new language that Christians speak, in their words and in their actions

As we've thought about the resurrection and what it means today, we've thought about an event that truly happened and made a difference. But we need to spell out that difference as fully and as freely as we can, in ways that address a culture in which, over the last century, various kinds of totalitarianism have pretended humanity is negotiable. The gospel of the resurrection speaks into that and against that. Humanity is not negotiable. It speaks into those places and environments of despair, where people don't believe that change is possible and don't believe that God's rule can already be real in the hearts and the lives of human beings. It speaks into an environment where people assume we're moving towards a death that is simply the end of every story, and our relation with God – if we have one – is just in this life. It speaks against a view of prayer that is anxious, fearful and takes for granted that God is a long way off. It speaks into and against an environment in which the body, the material world, is underrated and abused.

In all these ways Christ calls us to speak to a world that desperately needs the good news of the resurrection.

For reflection or discussion

1 How do you feel about the idea that the Bible illuminates the humanity of people from very diverse backgrounds?
2 How does belief in the resurrection show you that humanity can change? How does it help you to overcome your deepest fears?
3 How does it affect your prayer life? And your attitude to the material world?

Epilogue
The beginning of the new creation

For some people, when they first encounter an icon of the resurrection, it's just a little bit puzzling. There is Jesus descending to the dead, taking Adam and Eve by the hand, surrounded sometimes by prophets and kings of the old covenant. And it seems rather a long way from

Figure 1 Icon of the Resurrection, St Andrew Holborn

the resurrection narratives in the Gospels. Surely the resurrection is about those precious moments of personal encounter between the risen Jesus and his first disciples: those mysterious and elusive meetings that we considered in Chapter 4?

However, here in the icon in Figure 1, we're taken into another realm, another frame of reference. That of course is what an icon does: it takes you to the inner story, to the bedrock of what's going on. And what this icon says to us is that the bedrock of what is going on in the resurrection of Jesus Christ is the remaking of creation itself. Here are God and Adam and Eve: this is where it all began and this is where it begins again. The resurrection is not the happy ending of the story of Jesus: it's the story of the word of God speaking in the heart of darkness to bring life out of *nothing* and to bring the human race into existence as the carriers of his image and his likeness. That is what happened on Easter Sunday and what happens whenever Easter is re-enacted, commemorated afresh in the life of the believing community. It's why so often in the early Church – and today in the Eastern Church – Sunday is thought of as the 'eighth day' of the seven-day week. It's the start of the new world because it's the day of the resurrection of Christ.

> *What is going on in the resurrection of Jesus Christ is the remaking of creation itself*

So far, so good. The resurrection is the beginning of the new creation; the resurrection is the rising not only of Jesus, but of Adam and Eve. Then you look more closely at Adam and Eve in the icon, and you see that this is Adam and Eve *grown old*. They are not the radiant, naked figures of the first beginning of the story. Their faces are lined by suffering and experience, by guilt, by the knowledge of good and evil, scarred by life and by history. This is Adam and Eve having lost their innocence – the Adam and Eve who are of course ourselves, we who carry around with us the marks of history, of experience, of the knowledge of good and evil, hurts received and hurts done. Those are *our* faces on the icon, Adam and Eve 'four thousand winters' on, as the carol rightly puts it.[1] Because the history of Adam and Eve is a wintry one, and we know that in ourselves.

So when we speak of the resurrection as a new beginning, a new creation, it is in the sense that the risen Jesus reaches down and touches precisely *those* faces: Adam and Eve grown old. He doesn't wave a wand and make them young again, strip off their clothes and leave them standing in their first innocence. What he deals with is humanity as it has become, our humanity, suffering and struggling, failed and failing. The resurrection is not about the wiping out of our history, pain or failure, it is about how pain

---

[1] 'Adam lay y-bounden'.

and failure themselves – humanity marked by history – may yet be transfigured and made beautiful. Perhaps the most poignant feature of the icon is those aged faces: Adam and Eve four thousand years old in winter, turning to their spring, and being renewed.

So what the Christian gospel offers is indeed a new beginning. It is indeed something from nothing, life from death, light from darkness. And at the same time it is, mysteriously, the transformation of what we have become: real flesh and blood human beings with our histories, with the lines etched in our faces by those metaphorical four thousand winters. If we did not believe that, what a very strange and hopeless world we would inhabit: a world in which again and again, when we turned to God, we would have to write off what had become of us and say, 'All that is to be discarded,' and the tape simply reeled back to the beginning again. No: God 'wonderfully created us' as the prayer says, 'and yet more wonderfully restored us.'[2] The re-creation, the new beginning of resurrection, is *more* wonderful because it is the planting of newness and fresh-ness, beauty and vision and glory, in faces like yours and mine, in lives like yours and mine, in Adam and Eve as they are there depicted. And that is why the resurrection is good news for those in the midst of what seems to be

---

[2] From the Collect for the First Sunday after Christmas, *Common Worship*.

incurable, intractable pain or failure, in the middle of a world or an experience where, practically speaking, there seems so little hope. It's not that the risen Christ appears saying, 'By magic I will take away your history and I will smooth out your faces'; but that the risen Christ says, 'In the depth of this reality I will speak, I will be present and I will transform.'

There are many icons depicting the great saints of the classical era of Christianity, but there are also icons now of the saints of our own age, saints whose photographs we can see. And it's one of the most intriguing and challenging things you can imagine: to look at a *photograph* of someone whose *icon* you can also see. Any fool can take a photograph (within reasonable limitations!) but only someone living in the light of the resurrection can paint an icon. And it comes home when you see the lined, ordinary, prosaic faces of modern people who have been recognized as saints; when you see those faces transformed in modern icons to show the glory and radiance coming through their very specific, recognizable contemporary faces, it is then that you see something of what this image of the resurrection is telling us. It's *this* flesh and blood, *this* history, *these* sufferings and *these* failures that the risen Jesus touches and transfigures.

So, as we come to view this icon of the resurrection, this image of the new beginning, we are asked to look at

Adam and Eve as if in a mirror: to see there the ups and downs, lights and shadows of our own actual, complex, uneven lives, and to see that as the place where the risen Jesus begins. Because God begins always with *who* we are now and *what* we are now: and it's there, now, that life comes

> *We may begin again at every moment by the power and strength of the risen Jesus*

from death, and light from darkness. We may begin again at every moment by the power and strength of the risen Jesus. But more: that new beginning is also the gathering-together, the leading-forward of all that we actually are and have become.

May God give us the freedom and the courage to look into that mirror: that mirror of the wintry face, of Adam and Eve grown old; and in that moment to see something of how the spring begins in its heart: the spring of Jesus' own Easter, his rising, his 'eastering in us', as the poet Gerard Manley Hopkins says.

In him our life begins afresh day by day, because he is, and always will be, *God with us*.

To him be glory for ever and ever. Amen.

Acknowledgements

The first three chapters in this book are based on Holy Week addresses given in Canterbury in 2006.

Chapters 3 and 4 are based on the Bishop of Winchester's Lent Lectures, 2008.

The Epilogue was originally given as a sermon for a Parish Eucharist at St Andrew Holborn, London, during which a new icon of the resurrection (painted by a sister of the monastery of Vallechiara) was blessed. The icon is reproduced with kind permission of St Andrew Holborn.